Highlights

501
SPACE
JOKE-TIVITIES

Riddles, Puzzles, Fun Facts, Cartoons, Tongue Twisters, and Other Giggles!

HIGHLIGHTS PRESS
Honesdale, Pennsylvania

D1466158

MIXED-UP PLANETS

There are eight planets in our solar system. They are listed in order below, but their names are scrambled! Can you unscramble each set of letters to find each planet's name?

RYUMCRE _ _ _ _ _ _ _

USVEN _ _ _ _ _

HTAER _ _ _ _ _

RSMA _ _ _ _

JPRIUET _ _ _ _ _ _ _

AUSNRT _ _ _ _ _ _

RASUUN _ _ _ _ _ _

NEUPETN _ _ _ _ _ _ _

What did the atmosphere say to Earth?

I've got you covered.

FUN FACT

Researchers have found mathematical evidence supporting the existence of a hypothetical Neptune-sized planet orbiting far beyond Pluto.

PLANET X?

Can you name the planet shown in each photo?

  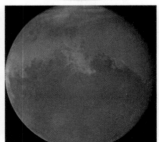 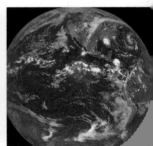

_____ _____ _____ _____

SOLAR SYSTEM SEARCH

Can you find the hidden objects in our solar system?

 boomerang

 button

 **wedge of cheese**

 heart

 ice-cream cone

 fish

 pear

 wedge of lemon

 mitten

 yo-yo

AMONG THE STARS

These **34** objects are found in space—and in this grid. All the words fit together in only one way. Use the number of letters in each word as a clue to where it might fit. We started you off with **VEGA**.

4 Letters

MARS
MOON
STAR
VEGA

5 Letters

COMET
EARTH
ORBIT
ORION
PLUTO
TITAN
VENUS

6 Letters

CASTOR
EUROPA
GALAXY
METEOR
NEBULA
PULSAR
SATURN
SIRIUS
TRITON
URANUS

7 Letters

JUPITER
MERCURY
NEPTUNE
PANDORA
SUNSPOT

8 Letters

ASTEROID
MILKY WAY
UNIVERSE

11 Letters

SOLAR SYSTEM

9 Letters

BIG DIPPER
BLACK HOLE
SUPERNOVA

12 Letters

SPACE STATION

What flowers grow in outer space?

sunflowers

5

IN THE STARS

There are **88** officially recognized constellations. Below is a list of every constellation and its description.

Andromeda – princess of Ethiopia

Antlia – air pump

Apus – bird of paradise

Aquarius – water bearer

Aquila – eagle

Ara – altar

Aries – ram

Auriga – charioteer

Boötes – plowman

Caelum – chisel or graving tool

Camelopardalis – giraffe

Cancer – crab

Canes Venatici – hunting dogs

Canis Major – big dog

Canis Minor – little dog

Capricornus – sea goat

Carina – keel of Argonauts' ship

Cassiopeia – queen of Ethiopia

Centaurus – centaur

Cepheus – king of Ethiopia

Cetus – sea monster or whale

Chamaeleon – chameleon

Circinus – compass

Columba – dove

Coma Berenices – Bernice's hair

Corona Australis – southern crown

Corona Borealis – northern crown

Corvus – crow

Crater – cup

Crux – southern cross

Cygnus – swan or northern cross

Delphinus – dolphin

Dorado – swordfish

Draco – dragon

Equuleus – little horse

Eridanus – river

Fornax – furnace

Gemini – twins

Grus – crane

Hercules – son of Zeus

Horologium – clock

Hydra – sea serpent

Hydrus – water snake

Indus – Indian

Lacerta – lizard

Leo – lion

Leo Minor – lesser lion

Lepus – hare

Libra – scales

Lupus – wolf

In the past, people made up stories about the shapes they saw in the stars. These became the constellations we know today.

Over half of these constellations are attributed to the ancient Greeks, who consolidated earlier astrological works by the ancient Babylonians, Egyptians, and Assyrians.

Lynx – lynx

Lyra – lyre or harp

Mensa – Table Mountain

Microscopium – microscope

Monoceros – unicorn

Musca – fly

Norma – carpenter's level

Octans – octant

Ophiuchus – serpent bearer

Orion – the hunter

Pavo – peacock

Pegasus – the winged horse

Perseus – hero who saved Andromeda

Phoenix – phoenix

Pictor – painter's easel

Pisces – fishes

Piscis Austrinus – southern fish

Puppis – stern of the Argonauts' ship

Pyxis – compass on the Argonauts' ship

Reticulum – net

Sagitta – arrow

Sagittarius – archer

Scorpius – scorpion

Sculptor – sculptor

Scutum – shield

Serpens – serpent

Sextans – sextant

Taurus – bull

Telescopium – telescope

Triangulum – triangle

Triangulum Australe – southern triangle

Tucana – toucan

Ursa Major – great bear

Ursa Minor – lesser bear

Vela – sail of the Argonauts' ship

Virgo – virgin

Volans – flying fish

Vulpecula – fox

Create your own constellation!
What's its story?

···· ☆ DRAW ☆ ····

a picture of it here.

☆ LAUGH ATTACK ☆

What is an astronaut's favorite place on the computer?

The space bar

What do space aliens eat for breakfast?

Flying sausages

What type of knot do you tie in outer space?

An astro-knot

Astronaut #1: What is a space creature's favorite dessert?
Astronaut #2: I don't know. What?
Astronaut #1: Martian-mellows.

How does an alien count to twenty-three?

On its fingers

What do astronauts like to eat for dinner?

Spaghetti and meteor-balls

What's an astronaut's favorite board game?

Moon-opoly

Why are astronauts successful people?

Because they always go up in the world

After landing on Earth, a space alien saw a bird. The alien asked, "How much does it cost to stay in a hotel?" "Cheep, cheep," said the bird. "Good," said the alien, "because it cost me a fortune to get here!"

What do you say to a two-headed space alien?

Hello, hello!

Why didn't the alien finish his homework?

He wasn't hungry.

SPACE ENCOUNTER

Can you find at least **15** differences between these two pictures?

LOOK UP!

There are **14** UFOs hidden in the grids below.
Here's how to figure out where they belong:

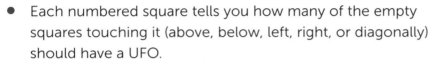

- Each numbered square tells you how many of the empty squares touching it (above, below, left, right, or diagonally) should have a UFO.
- Place an **X** on squares that can't have a UFO. Draw a UFO on squares that have one.

Hints:

- A UFO cannot go in a square that has a number.
- Put an **X** on all the squares touching a zero.
- In the big grid, start by putting an **X** on all the squares around the zero. That leaves seven possible squares around the 6 for the six UFOs. Use the other numbered squares to determine where those six UFOs go.

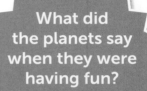

What did the planets say when they were having fun?

~~~

"This is Pluto-rrific!"

		3	
2			**2**
	2		
0			**0**

Where does an alien park its vehicle?

~~~

At a parking meteor.

	1				**1**
			2		
2					**1**
		6		**4**	
					2
0		**1**		**3**	

HOME SWEET HOME

Zig, Vot, and Spo are homesick. Can you use the clues to match each alien with the right spaceship and home planet? Use the chart to keep track of your answers. Put an **X** in each box that can't be true and an **O** in boxes that match.

	Hot Planet	Cold Planet	Wet Planet	Red Ship	Yellow Ship	Blue Ship
Zig						
Vot						
Spo						

CLUES:
1. The red spaceship came from a hot planet.
2. Vot's planet is cold, but not wet.
3. The yellow spaceship belongs to Spo.

TO THE MOON!

The National Air and Space Museum in Washington, DC, is home to the largest collection of historic aircraft and spacecraft in the world, including the command module of the first successful moon landing mission—Apollo 11.

FUN FACT

The Apollo 11 astronauts were Neil Armstrong, Michael Collins, and Edwin "Buzz" Aldrin.

How is an astronaut like a football player?

They both want to make touchdowns.

Find the letters in the illustration and fill in the picture code to read a message from the plaque that the Apollo 11 astronauts left on the Moon.

What do astronauts do when they're sorry?

They Apollo-gize.

WORD FOR WORDS

At approximately 2.5 million light-years away, the Andromeda galaxy is the closest galaxy to our Milky Way. Andromeda contains about one trillion stars. This galaxy also contains a lot of words. The letters in **ANDROMEDA** can be used to make many other words. Use the clues below to come up with some of them.

ANDROMEDA

1. A barrier that holds back water _____ _____ _____

2. You listen with this _____ _____ _____

3. Used to row a boat _____ _____ _____

4. A female horse _____ _____ _____ _____

5. To fix something _____ _____ _____ _____

6. To admire _____ _____ _____ _____ _____

7. A smell _____ _____ _____ _____

8. Spanish word for mother _____ _____ _____ _____

9. A Japanese noodle dish _____ _____ _____ _____

10. The opposite of orderly _____ _____ _____ _____ _____

FUN FACT

The Andromeda galaxy is the farthest object we can see with the naked eye. It looks dim from so far away and is easiest to find on moonless nights.

Who has the biggest phone bill in the galaxy?

E.T.

How do cows travel to the Moon?

They take the Milky Way.

How many galaxies do astronomers know of?

No one knows exactly how many galaxies the universe has. That's because most galaxies are much fainter than the Milky Way. If they're far away, even the best telescopes can't see them. However, astronomers can estimate how many there are.

Astronomers look at nearby space, where they can see all of the local galaxies. Then they assume that distant parts of the universe, which they can't see well, are similar. They know how big the observable universe is. It stretches 14 billion light-years in all directions from Earth. Then they estimate the total number of galaxies in all that space: between 100 billion and 200 billion.

FUN FACT

The 200-inch Hale Telescope is at the Palomar Observatory in San Diego County, California.

Of course, this number is uncertain. The true number could be a few times more or a few times less. But it's the best guess we have for now.

Which two scenes are exactly the same?

☆ LAUGH ATTACK ☆

What do you call deer in space?

Star bucks

What did Earth say to the Sun?

You light up my life.

What does one star say to another star when it passes by?

Nice to meteor.

What has rings but no fingers?

Saturn

Why did the alien cross the galaxy?

To get to the other side

Ben: Which planet is closest to us?
Winnie: I think it's Venus.
Ben: No, it's Earth!

How did Mary's little lamb get to Mars?

By rocket sheep

What do planets do for fun?

They sing Nep-tunes.

Astronaut #1: Let's go to the Moon.
Astronaut #2: We can't.
Astronaut #1: Why not?
Astronaut #2: It's a full Moon.

GIVE ME SPACE!

Test how much you know about space with this quiz.
If you can answer all the questions, give yourself a gold star!

1. Pluto is known as this.
a. A dwarf planet
b. A baby planet
c. A puppy planet

2. Which planet is closest to the Sun?
a. Mercury
b. Venus
c. Earth

3. How much bigger is the Sun's diameter than Earth's?
a. 19 times bigger
b. 109 times bigger
c. 19 million times bigger

4. What are Saturn's rings made up of?
a. Ice, dust, and rocks
b. Fiery gas
c. Gold and diamonds

5. A quasar is:
a. Far away and very bright
b. Far away and very dark
c. Afraid of the dark

6. What year did astronauts first walk on the Moon?
a. 1949
b. 1969
c. 1999

7. What is a common nickname for Mars?
a. The Red Planet
b. The Green Planet
c. E.T.'s Home Planet

Knock, knock.
Who's there?
Comet.
Comet who?
Comet open this door, please!

Knock, knock.
Who's there?
Comet.
Comet who?
Comet-y is hilarious!

SPACE RACE!

Soar from **START** to **FINISH** by zooming around the solar system. Find the way to go by answering each question correctly.

What are the solar system's favorite days of the week?

Saturn-day, Sunday, and Moon-day.

SKIM THE SURFACE

When visiting MERCURY, don't forget to take a

- bathing suit, because Mercury's surface has lots of oceans.
- pogo stick, because Mercury's surface has lots of craters.

CLOUDY WITH A CHANCE OF WHAT?

The thick clouds on VENUS are made of

- water, like the clouds on Earth.
- sulfuric acid, like the acid in batteries.

GRAND CANYON, MARS STYLE

If you raced the full length of the longest canyon on MARS, how far would you run?

- 2,500 miles
- 2.5 miles

GREEN-LIGHT IT

URANUS looks green because its air has

- methane gas.
- chlorophyll from plants.

SPACE BLING

Up close, you can see that SATURN'S beautiful rings are made mostly of

- water ice.
- stardust.

START

STAR LIGHT, STAR SO BRIGHT

How does the SUN make so much light? Tons of

solar-powered light bulbs

Nuclear reactions

AUGUST AWESOMENESS

Every August, particles hit EARTH's air and burn up, creating the Perseid meteor shower. These particles come from

a comet.

the Moon.

STILL STORMY

For more than 100 years, JUPITER has had a storm bigger than Earth itself. The storm is called the

Great Red Spot.

Orange Giant.

GOING IN CIRCLES?

Start the stopwatch! It takes this long for NEPTUNE to go once around the Sun:

365 days

165 years

MOON COUNT

How many moons go around little PLUTO?

Five

None

FINISH

19

WHAT'S WRONG?

Which things in this picture are silly? It's up to you!

What do you call a telescope that can't stop running into stuff?

A kaleidoscope

How did the astronomer feel about Orion's belt?

He thought it was a big waist of space.

KIDS' SCIENCE QUESTIONS

What's the difference between an asteroid and a meteor?

Asteroids are sometimes called minor planets. They are fairly small, rocky worlds. Like Earth and the other planets, asteroids move in orbits around the Sun. Most asteroids in our solar system are in a "belt"—a group of orbiting asteroids that lie between Mars and Jupiter.

A meteor is a much smaller bit of rock that enters Earth's atmosphere. As it falls through the air, it burns from the heat of friction. We see it as a streak of light in the sky.

Two other important terms are *meteoroid* and *meteorite*. A meteoroid is a bit of rock or a dust particle in space. When a meteoroid falls into Earth's atmosphere, it burns up, creating a meteor. When lots of meteoroids hit the air, we see a meteor shower. If a meteoroid doesn't burn up completely, the part that hits Earth's surface is called a meteorite.

What did the meteor mom say to her dirty son?

Take a meteor shower.

METEOR PUZZLE

There are multiple meteor showers you can view throughout the year. Write each set of colored letters on the same-colored lines to find out when some of the major meteor showers peak.

LPOLGQREUYEAERIODMORSRAINENTNINIIDIDIDSIDSDSDSSS

April _____

August _____

October _____

November _____

December _____

December/January _____

TIC TAC ROW

Each of these spaceships has something in common with the other two spaceships in the same row—across, down, and diagonally. For example, in the top row across, each spaceship has an antenna. Can you tell what's alike in each row?

☆ LAUGH ATTACK ☆

What should you do when you see a green alien?

Wait until it's ripe!

What is an alien's favorite candy?

Mars bars

What do you call a monkey in space?

A Moon baboon

How is food served in space?

On satellite dishes

LOVE IS IN THE ATMOSPHERE

Find these hidden objects in the picture. Then use the picture code to fill in the letters and finish the joke.

Where did the alien put her teacup?

On a flying saucer

A	E	L	O	U	V	Y	Z
fishhook	baseball bat	comb	sock	domino	ice-cream cone	cookie	button

What did the three-eyed alien say to her sweetheart?

"eye, eye, eye love you!"

23

MOON LANDING

Can you find at least **19** differences between these two photos?

FUN FACT

Astronauts first landed on the Moon on July 20, 1969.

Try to say these

☆ TONGUE TWISTERS ☆

three times, fast.

The Moon's magnificence moved Maggie.

Shane stares at shining stars.

FUN FACT

The word *lunar*, which describes something related to a moon, comes from the Latin word *luna*, which means "moon."

SPACED OUT

It's time for Planet Zongo's annual spaceship parade, but it looks like some folks bought their spaceships at the same place. Can you find the three pairs of spaceships that match exactly? Then, try to say the tongue twisters three times, fast.

What's the best month for a spaceship parade?

March

TONGUE TWISTERS

Eight aliens ate eighty almonds.

Spa's spaceship started, then stopped.

KIDS' SCIENCE QUESTIONS

Why is there no gravity in space?

Gravity is strongest when objects are close together and have a lot of mass. Out in space, there is mostly . . . space! So even massive objects can be too far apart to be affected by one another's gravity. Yet some are close enough. For example, Earth is held in orbit by the Sun's gravity, and the Moon is held in orbit by Earth's gravity.

Astronauts orbiting Earth are within the pull of Earth's gravity, too. But they feel weightless because their spacecraft is racing around Earth. You might feel the same way on a downhill roller coaster.

WHEEE!

A little planet broke out of orbit and raced around the Sun and Moon. "What are you doing?" her mother called. "Look, Mom," shouted the little planet, "no gravities!"

CHECK... AND DOUBLE CHECK

Compare these two pictures. Can you find at least **12** differences?

✩ LAUGH ATTACK ✩

What is the center of gravity?
The letter v

What keeps jazz musicians on the ground?
Groove-ity

What's the difference between an astronaut and a float?
An astronaut can float, but a float can't astronaut.

What do astronauts put on their turkey?
Gravy-ty

What do astronauts like to drink?
Gravi-tea

I'm reading a book about anti-gravity. I can't put it down!

Up or Down?

When astronauts are out in space,
what's up or down is a puzzling case.

Their feet are up. Or are they down?
Is right-side up *and* upside down?

If up is down and down is up,
is upside down now right-side up?

Down or up, up or down,
they're glad to get back on the ground.

COUNTDOWN TO LAUNCH

These **41** space terms fit together in the grid in only one way. Use the number of letters in each word as a clue to where it might fit. We started you off with **ROCKET**. Once you fill them in, unscramble the highlighted letters to find the answer to the riddle.

4 Letters
CREW
FUEL
MOON
TEST

5 Letters
EAGLE
EARTH
ORBIT
SOYUZ
SPACE

6 Letters
APOLLO
CLOUDS
GEMINI
LAUNCH
METEOR
OXYGEN
PLANET
ROCKET
SKYLAB
STAGES
STARRY
STRAIN

7 Letters
AIRLOCK
CONTROL
DOCKING
ECLIPSE
GRAVITY
MERCURY
MISSION
SHUTTLE

8 Letters
BLAST OFF

9 Letters
ASTEROIDS
ASTRONAUT
ASTRONOMY
DISCOVERY
HALF-LIGHT
SATELLITE
SPACEWALK

10 Letters
ATMOSPHERE
EXPEDITION
SPACECRAFT
TRAJECTORY

Why did the astronaut smile during takeoff?

___ ___ ___ ___   ___ ___ ___ ___ ___   ___ ___ ___   ___ ___ ___ ___ ___ ___ .

☆ TONGUE TWISTERS ☆

three times, fast.

Surely Shirley should start to study stars.

Lana and Luna had lunch before launch.

Rita readied the wrong rocket.

Reese's rocket really rocks!

R O C K E T

READING SPACE

Follow each line from a letter to a blank space. Write the letter in that space to find the answer to the riddle.

What do astronauts like to read?

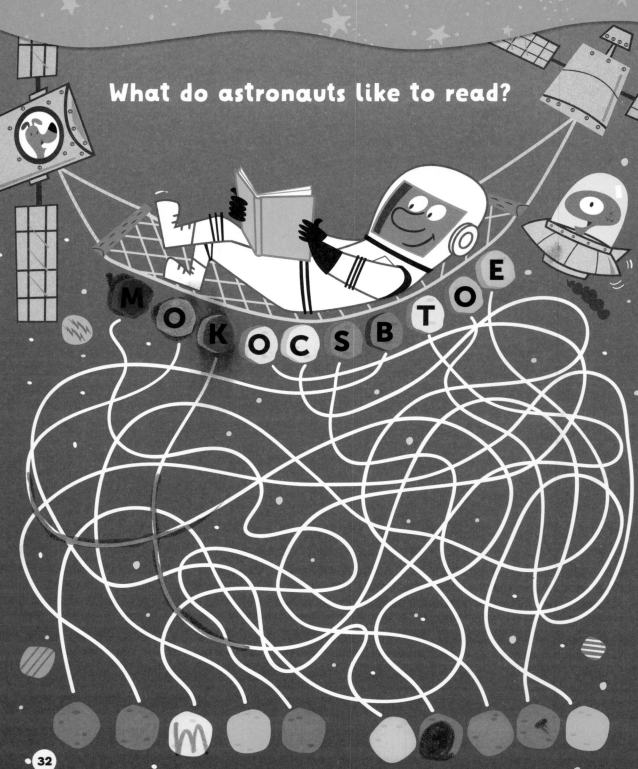

HELP THE CARTOONIST!

These cartoons are missing their captions. Write your own punch lines.

A visitor goes into an astronomy museum.

Visitor: How old is the universe?

Tour Guide: It's 13.8 billion and 11 years old.

Visitor: How do you know the age so precisely?

Tour Guide: Well, when I was first hired, an astronomer told me that the universe is 13.8 billion years old, and I've worked here for 11 years.

STELLA'S SOUVENIRS

Stella has a souvenir for everyone. Can you find the hidden objects in this scene?
The hidden objects are also hidden words in this word search. Can you find them
in the grid below? We found the first one for you.

yo-yo

pizza

candy

hairbrush   key

cup

ruler

✓ football

☆ LAUGH ATTACK ☆

What is the Moon worth?
$1.00, because it has four quarters.

What's an astronaut's favorite snack?
A Moonpie

e	t	q	q	r	u	l	e	r	s
n	f	o	o	t	b	a	l	l	a
o	c	i	s	p	i	d	e	r	l
c	p	f	s	v	y	l	a	e	t
m	u	b	y	h	i	t	b	d	s
a	c	q	d	c	w	h	t	d	h
e	w	b	n	u	a	a	e	a	a
r	k	e	a	i	a	i	n	l	k
c	p	e	c	j	n	r	v	p	e
e	i	v	y	m	a	b	e	t	r
c	p	s	j	r	n	r	l	s	c
i	o	y	o	y	a	u	o	l	e
k	a	u	r	q	b	s	p	g	b
a	z	z	i	p	j	h	e	p	l

fish

saltshaker

ladder

ice-cream cone

banana

envelope

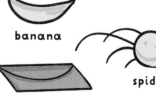

spider

pencil

☆ LAUGH ATTACK ☆

Knock, knock.
Who's there?
Saturn.
Saturn who?
Saturn my phone and now it won't work.

How does the Man in the Moon get his hair cut?
Eclipse it

Knock, knock.
Who's there?
Jupiter.
Jupiter who?
Jupiter fly in my soup?

What did the dentist call the astronaut's cavity?
A black hole

Where does a fish blast off to?
Trout-er space

What did one flying pig say to the other?
"Don't hog all the space."

Why is the Sun brighter in Hollywood?
Because it's a star.

Knock, knock.
Who's there?
Comet.
Comet who?
Comet a crime, go to jail.

What did the comet say to the sun?
See you next time around!

What do you like about your job?

I like having my own space.

SPACE PUZZLER

We're blasting off to outer space, but we forgot to pack our vowels!
Can you figure out each of these space-related words?

1. **ECLPS** __ __ __ __ __ ▢ __

2. **JPTR** __ __ __ __ __ __

3. **PLNT** __ __ __ __ ▢ __

4. **GLXY** __ __ ▢ __ __ __

5. **STRN** __ __ __ ▢ __ __

6. **BLCK HL** __ __ ▢ __ __   __ __ __ __

7. **SLR FLR** __ __ __ __ __   __ __ ▢ __

8. **SLR SYSTM** __ __ __ __ __ ▢ __ __ __ __ __

9. **CMT** __ __ ▢ __ __

10. **BG DPPR** __ __ __   __ __ __ __ __ __

Write the highlighted letters in order on the spaces below to solve the riddle.

How does the solar system tell jokes?

With a lot of __ __ __ __ __ __ __ __ __

37

FAMILY TRIP

Each blue word in the silly story is also a hidden object.
After you read the story, find the objects
in the big picture on the next page.

Please excuse my **SAILBOAT** from school tomorrow. As you may know, our **SOCK** family was recently contacted by the head **SLICE OF PIZZA** at NASA and asked to participate in a space/time experiment. So we and our pet **WEDGE OF LEMON** and **GOLF CLUB** will be traveling **NEEDLE** years into the future tomorrow. We will probably end up on the planet **CANDY CANE**-20 in the Alpha-**BOWL** solar system in the **DINOSAUR** galaxy. By the way, all the teachers there happen to be **HOCKEY STICK**s with five **FISHHOOK**s and 20 **TRAFFIC LIGHT**s! You would so fit in!

It will certainly be a **FISH** experience, and I hope you agree. The plan is for my **BELL** to bring some **LADLE**s back from the trip for **FLAG**-and-Tell at school. If all goes well, my **FLASHLIGHT** should be back in school by **RING**!

Thank you.

ROCKET DRAW

Follow these steps to draw a rocket on the next page.
Or use your imagination to draw your own rocket.

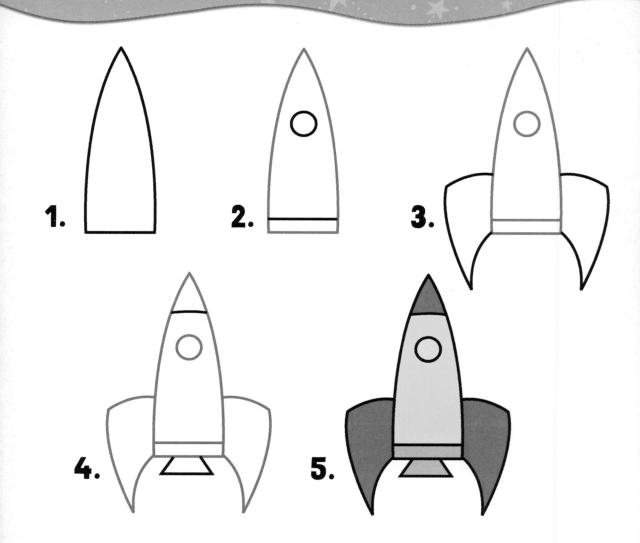

1. 2. 3.

4. 5.

Try to say these

☆ TONGUE TWISTERS ☆

three times, fast.

Sam sold Susie seven spaceships.

Robbie rode a ruby rocket.

Chaz chews chocolate chips on spaceships.

Knock, knock.
Who's there?
Rocket.
Rocket who?
Rocket the boat anymore, and we'll all fall in!

What time is it when a rocket ship has its second meal of the day?

Launch-time

Which frontiersman loved space?

Davy Rockett

ASTRO ADVENTURE

Find your way through the Imagination Constellations from **START** to **FINISH**. Be sure to avoid the satellites along the way. Then solve the word puzzles.

START

Are there more blue (hotter) stars or red (cooler) stars?

RIDDLE 1:
When will pigs fly into space?

RIDDLE 2:
How do you get a baby astronaut to fall asleep?

RIDDLE 3:
Why did the Moon stop eating?

RIDDLE 4:
What do astronauts eat for breakfast?

FINISH

Unscramble this word to find out what kind of puzzle solver you are.

L A R S T E L !

If an astronaut is in space, how does he or she use one of those jet packs?

Those jet packs work as life preservers. If an astronaut's tether breaks during a space walk, that person could be in great danger. But he or she could use the jet pack to get back to safety.

The jet pack holds tanks of harmless nitrogen gas. It has 24 nozzles for shooting out jets of the gas in different directions. The astronaut can use the joystick and other controls to release bursts of gas and move back to the safety of a spacecraft or space station.

Why do astronauts wear white space suits?

According to NASA, there are two reasons why astronauts wear white. First, white helps keep astronauts cool. Dark colors absorb a lot of light, which changes from light energy to heat energy. White avoids a lot of that heat by reflecting the light away.

Second, white stands out against the black sky. When astronauts are working outside their spacecraft, the other astronauts can see them easily.

What did the astronaut say about her trip to space?

It was out of this world!

Which two astronauts are the same?

MISSION CONTROL

Welcome to the Mission Control Center at Johnson Space Center in Houston, Texas! Can you find at least **20** differences between these two pictures?

Which two robotic landers are exactly the same?

What did the astronaut say to his boss when he tripped?

That is one small step, foreman.

FLOAT ON

There are **5** objects hidden in the scene on the next page. Write each set of colored letters on the same-colored lines to figure out the hidden objects, then find them in the scene!

FSRSFPYSUAIPNPTNONOUGNELOPGLAANEN

_____

_____

_____

_____

_____

Which two views of Earth are exactly the same?

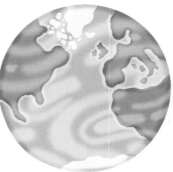

FUN FACT

The name *Earth* comes from old English and Germanic words that mean "ground." It is the only planet that isn't named after Greek or Roman gods or goddesses.

MOON WALK

Twelve men have walked on the Moon. Their names can fit in the grid in just one way. Use the number of letters in each person's name as a clue to where it might fit. We started you off with **JOHN YOUNG**.

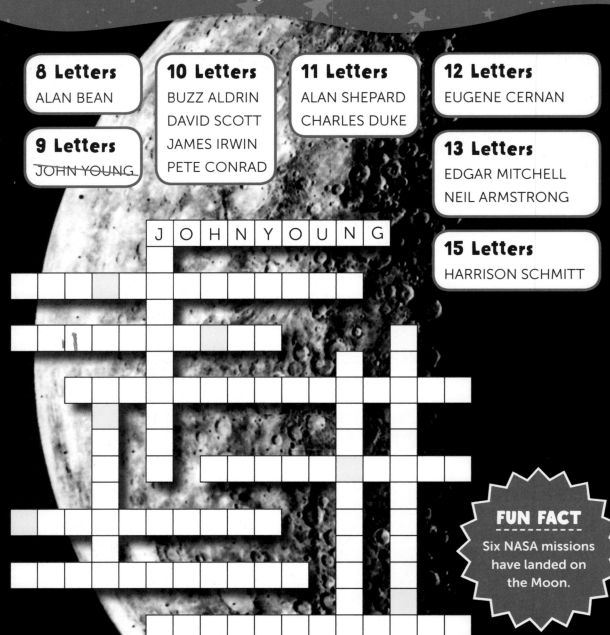

8 Letters
ALAN BEAN

9 Letters
~~JOHN YOUNG~~

10 Letters
BUZZ ALDRIN
DAVID SCOTT
JAMES IRWIN
PETE CONRAD

11 Letters
ALAN SHEPARD
CHARLES DUKE

12 Letters
EUGENE CERNAN

13 Letters
EDGAR MITCHELL
NEIL ARMSTRONG

15 Letters
HARRISON SCHMITT

J O H N Y O U N G

FUN FACT
Six NASA missions have landed on the Moon.

Unscramble the six shaded letters to spell the name of the space program that sent these men to the Moon.

— — — — — —

A NOTE TO MOM ON MOONWALK DAY

I'm building a spacecraft in the yard
and I'll be leaving soon.
Like astronaut Neil Armstrong,
I'm heading to the Moon.
And yes—I have my toothbrush.
And yes—I'll comb my hair.
I've packed a nice warm blanket
and a change of underwear.
I'll bring you back a Moon rock,
but because I'm a beginner,
the trip could take some extra time.
I might be late for dinner.

SPACE WALK

Alice is ready to float back to the space station. Which path will take her there?

Try to say these

☆ TONGUE TWISTERS ☆

three times, fast.

Fred, from Florida, floats freely.

Spencer swiftly spun the space station.

Wendy wobbled once.

FINISH

51

WHAT'S WRONG?

Which things in this picture are silly? It's up to you!

✸ LAUGH ATTACK ✸

3 books never written:
Volcanoes
by Anne E. Ruption

A Guide to Earth's Rocks
by G. O. Logical

How to Save the World
by Justin Time

FUN FACT

There are lots of volcanoes in space! In addition to Earth, the planets Mercury, Venus, and Mars all bear the scars of volcanoes.

What is a volcano's favorite food?

Lavacados

A BRIGHT MEETING

To find the answer to the riddle below, first cross out all the pairs of matching letters. Then write the remaining letters in order in the spaces beneath the riddle.

SS   BB   LL   IM   QQ   CC   TT

VE   DD   XX   EE   OO   RY   JJ

NN   WW   II   PL   ZZ   AA   KK

UU   EA   SS   LL   HH   OO   SE

RR   DD   DT   VV   EE   II   MM

YY   UU   OO   OH   PP   CC   EA

GG   TT   TY   AA   KK   OU   EE

What did the Sun say when it was introduced to Earth?

In very _____ _____ _____ _____ _____ .

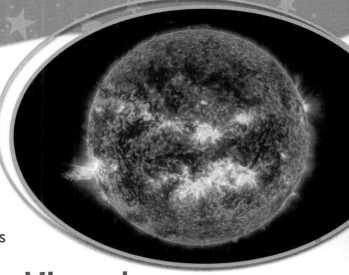

How does the Sun light up?

The Sun is releasing energy, which we see in the form of light and feel in the form of heat. The Sun is made up mostly of hydrogen. On Earth, hydrogen is a light gas. But the Sun is so large that its gravity packs all that hydrogen together and heats it to several million degrees at its center.

All that heat causes a reaction in which hydrogen is changing into another element, helium. That nuclear reaction results in a small loss in mass and the production of a great amount of energy. So we say the Sun "shines," which just means that it produces energy in the form of light.

The Sun always lights up when it gets a compliment!

Where does wind come from?

The Sun! Well, wind doesn't travel from the Sun, but light rays do, and they help create wind on Earth. Wind is basically just the movement of a bunch of air in the same general direction. Differences in air pressure and temperature, caused by the Sun, get it going.

Because of the way Earth rotates, solar light rays heat some parts of Earth's surface more than others. Air at hot spots rises and expands, leaving low pressure beneath it. Air at cold areas cools and falls, creating high pressure.

When high-pressure air rushes into a low-pressure area, that rush of air is wind. So the next time your umbrella gets blown inside out on a windy day, you'll know exactly what's to blame: the Sun!

SPACEY SUPERCHALLENGE!

The Air and Space Museum is busy today! There are 30 objects hidden in this scene. Without clues or knowing what to look for, can you find them all?

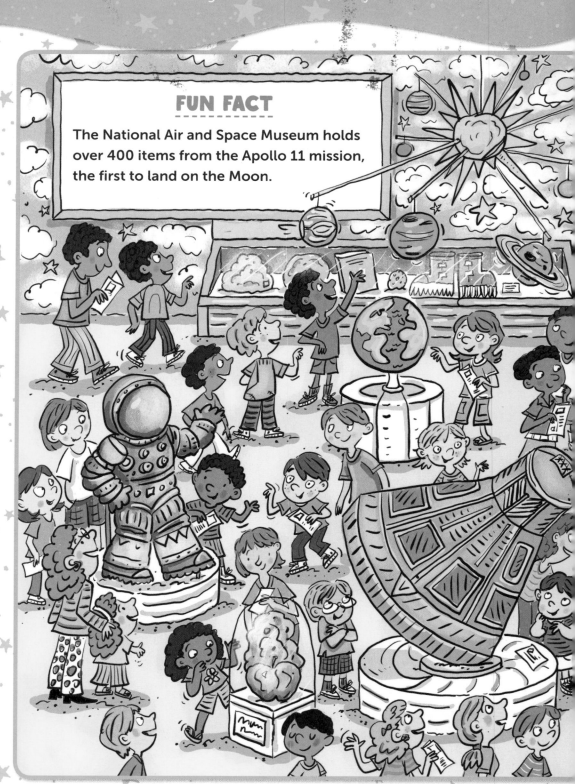

FUN FACT

The National Air and Space Museum holds over 400 items from the Apollo 11 mission, the first to land on the Moon.

☆ LAUGH ATTACK ☆

What kind of music do they play on a space shuttle?

Rocket roll

Why is it so hard to build a spaceship?

The price is astronomical.

SCRAMBLED SPACE

We've jumbled the names of **9** space-related words. Can you unscramble each set of letters and find the words? Once you have them all, read down the column of boxes to learn the answer to the riddle.

What do you get when you cross a galaxy and a toad?

RAMS   _ _ _ □

METCO   _ _ _ _ □

UNRATS   _ _ □ _ _ _

RITBO   _ _ □ _ _

LYMIK YAW   _ _ _ _ _ □ _ _

CLABK LOEH   _ _ _ _ □ _ _ _ _

TIPJUER   _ _ _ _ _ _ □

DREATSIO   _ _ _ □ _ _ _ _

SNUVE   _ _ _ _ □

How do astronomers discover other galaxies?

There are different ways astronomers find galaxies among the many objects in the sky. Here are a few of them.

If an object shows as a point of light, it's probably a star, not a galaxy. If the object has a pinwheel shape, it's a galaxy. Each galaxy is made up of many stars swirling around. So only a galaxy can take this shape.

If the object is a fuzzy patch of light, it might be a galaxy. Astronomers study its light to find out whether it's made up of stars and to measure how fast it's moving. If it's going faster than 500 kilometers per second, then it's probably a galaxy. It can't be part of our galaxy because it's moving too fast for the galaxy to hold it. So, if it's that far away and still bright enough to see, it's probably a galaxy itself.

But astronomers still make mistakes. They may think a galaxy is a star at first, if it's compact.

Before Galileo discovered Jupiter in 1610, what was the largest planet in the solar system?

Jupiter—it just wasn't discovered yet.

FUN FACT

M33, also known as the Triangulum galaxy, is about 2.9 million light-years away from Earth. It is located in the Triangulum constellation.

RIDDLE SUDOKU

Our Sudoku puzzles use letters instead of numbers. Fill in the squares so that the six letters appear only once in each row, column, and 2 x 3 box. Then read the yellow squares to find out the answer to the riddle.

RIDDLE: What is an astronaut's favorite meal?

Letters: **A C H L N U**

				N	
		C		U	
H	N				
				H	U
	H		A		
	C			L	

ANSWER:

___ ___ ___ ___ ___ ___

SAME SPACESHIPS

Can you find the two spaceships that are the same?

Try to say these

☆ TONGUE TWISTERS ☆

three times, fast.

Carlos cruised across the cosmos.

Riley Ryan rides a rocket.

Stella studied stars studiously.

SPACED OUT

Can you find at least **20** differences between these two photos?

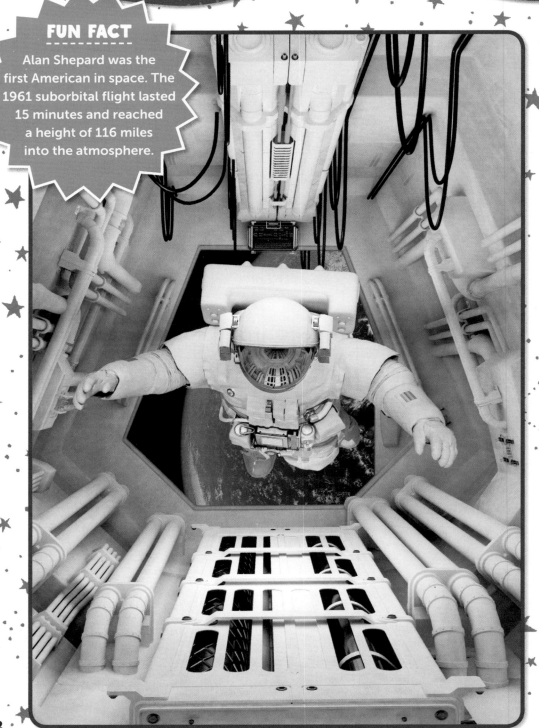

FUN FACT

Alan Shepard was the first American in space. The 1961 suborbital flight lasted 15 minutes and reached a height of 116 miles into the atmosphere.

☆ LAUGH ATTACK ☆

What sport do astronauts play?
Space-ball

Where do astronauts go to study?
The Moon-iversity

Why did the mouse-tronaut quit the space program?
He found out that the Moon isn't made of cheese.

FUN FACT

John Glenn was the first American to orbit Earth, in 1962. In 1998, he became the oldest astronaut to go to space, at 77.

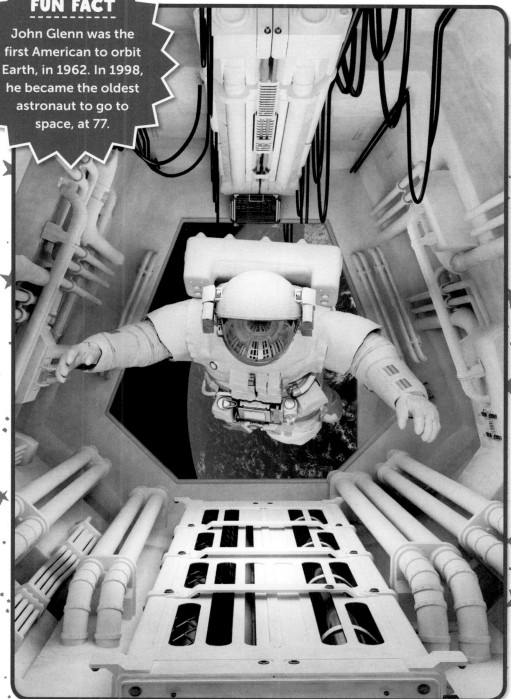

STAR SEARCH

Can you find these **8** jigsaw pieces in this photo of a nebula?

FUN FACT

A nebula is a giant cloud of gas and dust in space.

Try to say these

TONGUE ☆ TWISTERS ☆

three times, fast.

Shining, shimmering, silver stars.

Nelly named ninety-nine nebulae.

In outer space spin great galaxies.

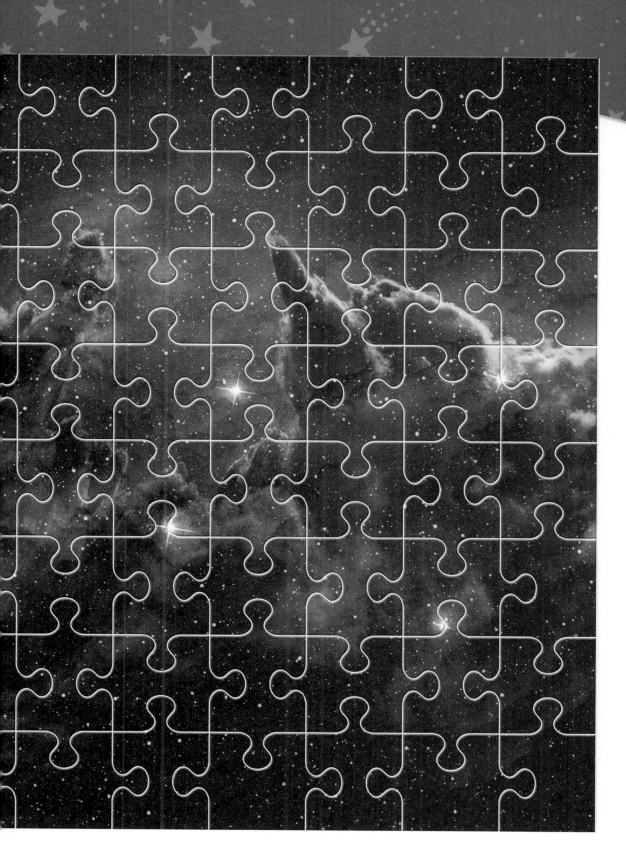

STARRY NIGHT

It's a great night to stargaze. Without clues or knowing what to look for, can you find the **13** objects hidden in this scene?

What kind of stars wear sunglasses?

Movie stars

How many stars are in the sky?

No one knows how many stars there are. The total number of stars is so large the best we can do is estimate the number.

Before the invention of the telescope, astronomers counted the stars. On a clear night, far from pollution and city lights, we can see 2,000 to 3,000 stars.

Using telescopes, astronomers have learned that the Sun is one of more than 100 billion (100,000,000,000) stars in our galaxy, the Milky Way. And they have found hundreds of billions of galaxies, each made up of billions of stars.

How does a star twinkle?

The light given off by a star is clear and steady. But most of the stars are so far away that we see them as only a tiny point of light. When the light reaches Earth, it passes through many layers of air. Some of the layers are cool and some are warm. When the light from the stars travels through those layers of air, the light is bent back and forth. That makes it look as if the stars are twinkling.

☆ LAUGH ATTACK ☆

What are the clumsiest things in the galaxy?
Falling stars

What do aliens put on their toast?
Space jam

What do alien artists paint?
Mars-terpieces

What did the Sun say to the Moon?
Looks like it's my night off.

How many astronomers does it take to change a light bulb?
None. Astronomers aren't scared of the dark.

When do astronauts knit and crochet?
On space craft night

ZOOM TO THE MOON!

Luna and Buzz are traveling to the Moon!
Blast from **START** to **FINISH** by answering each question correctly.

START

Magnets

Gravity

STUCK ON EARTH

You can't just jump off Earth. What holds you down?

TAKE A DEEP BREATH

You have to make sure your spaceship contains the same gases you breathe on Earth. What are the two most common gases in Earth's air?

Nitrogen and oxygen

Oxygen and carbon dioxide

FREE LIGHT SHOW

You see dust particles from space burning up in the air. They produce streaks of light called

comets.

meteors.

sunscreen

ozone gas

SUN-BELIEVABLE!

As you soar high above Earth, you pass through a substance called _____ that blocks the Sun's deadly ultraviolet light.

About a day

AROUND THE WORLD

How long does the Moon take to go around Earth once?

About a month

THAT'S SPIN-TERESTING

Earth spins once a day. How long does the Moon take to spin once?

Trick question! The Moon doesn't spin.

About a month— the same amount of time the Moon takes to go around Earth.

The Moon is bigger than Earth.

The Moon is smaller than Earth.

GET OUT YOUR TAPE MEASURE

You've made it to the Moon! How does its size compare to Earth's?

Nothing at all

$\frac{1}{6}$ of what you weigh on Earth

SPACE SCALE

How much will you weigh on the Moon?

LONG-DISTANCE VOYAGER

You've decided your next trip will be to the Sun! If it took one day to get to the Moon, how long would it take to get to the Sun, going at the same speed?

About 2 days

About 400 days

FINISH

CROSSWORD IN SPACE

Explore new frontiers with **54** clues about space in this puzzle. If you don't know the answer to a clue, look at the other clues that are around it, both across and down, or try another part of the puzzle and come back to the tough clue later. We did one for you.

Across

1 Daylight source
4 Mars is called the _____ Planet
7 _____ Bang (theory of how the universe started)
10 "One" in Spanish or Italian
11 "A long, long time _____"
12 From _____ _____ Z (2 words)
13 ". . . then Snow White _____ into the apple."
14 Helium balloons are often made of this material
16 The Sun is this type of celestial body
18 Venus or Mars, for example
21 "You can _____ your bottom dollar!"
23 Large container for liquid, usually with a spigot; a coffee _____
24 Continuously move around a star or planet
27 Halley's _____ ; heavenly streaker with a tail
29 _____ Grande
30 _____ Quixote
31 The Milky Way is one
34 Destination for Apollo 11
38 Not outgoing; shy
40 "That's _____ small step for man . . ."
41 A chimpanzee or gorilla is one
43 "Is that a yes or _____ _____?" (2 words)
44 Abbreviation for personal computers
45 Nickname for Theodore
46 Abbreviation for sergeant
47 "Get ready, get _____ , go!"

Down

1 Long deli sandwiches
2 One _____ of measurement is an inch
3 "_____ _____ chance!" (2 words)
4 Male sheep
5 Land of the pyramids
6 Toy baby
7 Ringling Bros. and _____ & Bailey Circus
8 "Tag, you're _____!"
9 Opposite of stop
15 Small battery size, but not the smallest
17 Abbreviation for a baseball statistic
19 It means "before" in poetry
20 Acronym for an explosive
22 "_____, phone home!"
24 Abbreviation for organization
25 Abbreviation for rich Internet application
26 Securely fastened; "I _____ the door."
27 Abbreviation for Denver's state
28 Letters between *L* and *P*, backward
30 "I really, really want to go to the party. I'm just _____ to go!"
32 Abbreviation for *artificial intelligence*
33 Shortened way to write Christmas
35 What you might say if you make a minor mistake
36 First word in a fairy tale
37 Cozy home for birds
39 Polka _____
41 All _____ once
42 Abbreviation for *physical education*

Unscramble the highlighted letters to find the answer to the riddle.

What's on the breakfast menu at a space restaurant?

___   ___ ___ ___ ___   ___ ___ ___ ___ ___

SPACE CODE

There are three jokes about space on this page. Use the picture code to fill in the letters and finish the jokes.

FUN FACT

Temperatures on the Moon range from as hot as 260°F when sunlight hits the surface to as cold as −280°F when the Sun goes down.

A

C

D

F

E

G

I

L

N

O

P

R

FUN FACT

The average distance between Earth and the Moon is 238,900 miles.

72

S T U Y

What do you call a magician from outer space?

A F L Y i N G

S o r c e r e r

What do you call a pecan in a spaceship?

How did the rocket lose its job?

UNICORNS IN SPACE

Starlight, Moonbeam, and Comet have made a new friend.
Can you find the hidden objects in this scene?

slice of
bread

fried egg

domino

sock

bow

bottle cap

nail

wedge of orange

Why does the Moon have craters?

Most of the craters we see on the Moon were made billions of years ago as the solar system was forming. During that time, the solar system had many more space rocks (asteroids) than it has now. They smashed into one another and into the moons and planets, and they often made craters where they hit.

Scientists say that Earth also had a lot of craters at that time. But the crust on Earth is always moving and changing, so the oldest craters have been erased.

How do astronauts say goodbye?

"See you later, crater!"

MOON SNACK

To find the answer to the riddle below, first cross out all the pairs of matching letters. Then write the remaining letters in order in the spaces beneath the riddle.

TT	NN	CR	PP	AA	GG
FF	XX	WW	YY	AT	HH
LL	CC	RR	BB	TT	ER
TA	MM	KK	SS	DD	HH
OO	FF	TE	II	QQ	UU
JJ	RS	VV	AA	RR	YY

What do Moon people call french fries?

crater

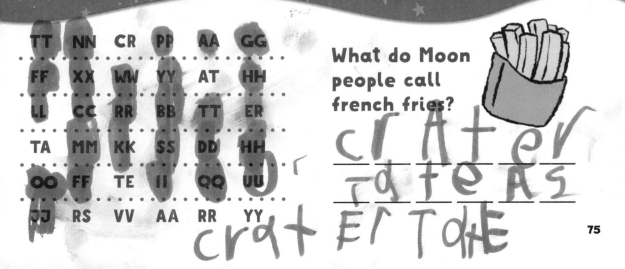

SPARKLING MAPS

Constellations
in the sky.
Sparkling figures
way up high.

Navigators
long ago
used these patterned
stars to know

their position
in the night,
the way toward home
etched in light.

What do you see in the sky?

☆ Navigate by the Stars ☆

Observing the stars to find a path is one of the first ways that people used the oldest science: **astronomy**. Know which way to go before starting out on a starlit adventure.

1. Find the Big Dipper.

2. Identify the two pointer stars. Draw an imaginary line between them.

Pointer Stars

☆ LAUGH ☆ ATTACK

Where do stars go to study?
Universe-ity

What letter will set a star in motion?
The letter T makes a star start.

How are false teeth like stars?
They both come out at night.

What did the astronomy professor tell her brightest student?
"You're my star pupil."

What does everyone who enters an astronomy competition get for participating?
Constellation prizes

What did the Mama Star say to the Papa Star?
"Isn't Junior bright?"

North Star

3. Extend the line upward. The first bright star you come to is the North Star, Polaris.

4. If you are facing the North Star, then north is in front of you, south is behind you, east is on your right, and west is on your left.

5, 4, 3, 2, 1 . . .

Inside this rocket are **34** space terms. Circle all the words that you find, up, down, across, backwards, and diagonally. We circled one word to get you started. When you are finished, write the leftover letters in order in the spaces below the rocket. They will give you an important message from mission control.

Word List

APOGEE
ARMS
ASTRONAUTS
ATOMIC
BOOSTERS
CAPE CANAVERAL
CAPSULES
CARGO
CELESTIAL
CONTROL
COSMOS
FAIL-SAFE
FORCE
FUNDED
GUIDANCE SYSTEMS
LANDER
MANNED SPACESHIP
MISSION

MOMENTUM
MOONS
MOUNTAIN
NECK-WRENCHING
 G-FORCES
NOSE CONE
ORBIT
PERIGEE
RAMJET
RANGER
REENTRY
SALVO
SPLASHDOWN
SPACE DEBRIS
THRUSTER
ZERO
ZOOM

What's as big as a rocket but weighs nothing?

Its shadow

78

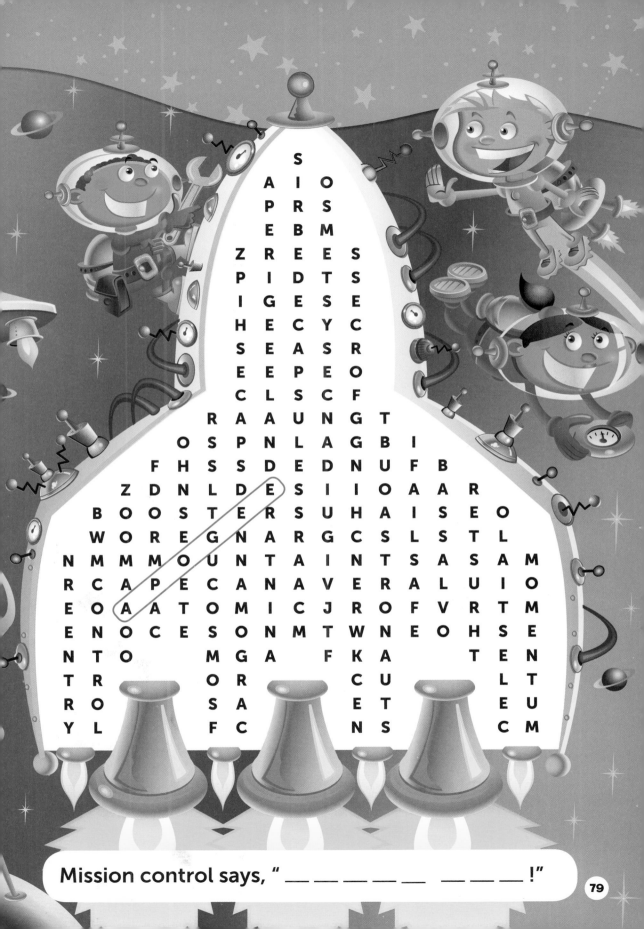

Mission control says, "_ _ _ _ _ _ _ _ _ !"

TIC TAC ROW

Each of these planets has something in common with the other two planets in the same row—across, down, and diagonally. For example, in the top row across, each planet has red spots. Can you tell what's alike in each row?

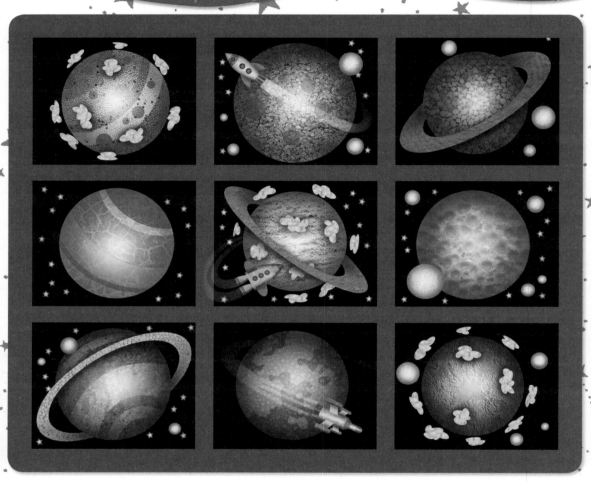

☆ LAUGH ATTACK ☆

What do you call a really fast planet?

Blur-cury

What do kids in space play with?

Pluto-yos

Knock, knock.
Who's there?
Venus.
Venus who?
Venus discuss the best way to launch this spaceship.

Why is Pluto not classified as a planet anymore?

Scientists have argued for years about whether Pluto should be called a planet. In 1930, when Pluto was discovered, it seemed to be alone. But in the 1990s, astronomers found lots of smaller objects beyond Neptune's orbit. These objects make up what is now known as the Kuiper Belt, or sometimes the Edgeworth-Kuiper Belt. Because Pluto is not alone out there, its status as a planet was called into question.

In August 2006, the International Astronomical Union defined three criteria for a full-sized planet:

1. It is in orbit around the Sun.
2. It has sufficient mass to assume hydrostatic equilibrium (a nearly round shape).
3. It has "cleared the neighborhood" around its orbit.

Clearing the neighborhood means that a planet has become gravitationally dominant— there are no other bodies of a similar size in its orbital area, other than its own satellites. Pluto meets the first two criteria, but because it shares its space with other objects in the Kuiper Belt it does not meet the third. For this reason, Pluto was reclassified as a dwarf planet.

> **FUN FACT**
>
> In 2015, the New Horizons spacecraft flew past Pluto and sent back the first-ever detailed photos of the dwarf planet.

> **FUN FACT**
>
> The heart-shaped feature on Pluto's surface was first seen in these detailed photos. It was named Tombaugh Regio, after Clyde Tombaugh, the discoverer of Pluto.

> **FUN FACT**
>
> The Kuiper Belt is 20 times as wide and 20 to 200 times as massive as the Asteroid Belt.

HIDDEN WORDS

There are **6** words hidden in the scene on the next page. Write each set
of colored letters on the same-colored lines to figure out the hidden words.
Then find them in the scene!

EMSCOSEMLRTUTOIBAEOPNIRONSTRE

_____

_____

_____

_____

_____

_____

KIDS' SCIENCE QUESTIONS

How does a telescope work?

To understand how a basic telescope makes faraway things look closer, think about why we can't see distant objects using only our eyes. First, the tiny opening at the front of the eye (the pupil) does not let in enough light to give many details of a distant object. Second, an object that's far away projects only a tiny picture onto the back of the eye.

A telescope improves our vision in two steps. First, the big end of the telescope gathers a lot of light from the object we're seeing. The lens in that end of the telescope focuses the light to make a small, bright image. Second, the small lens in the eyepiece magnifies that small image, spreading it over a bigger area on the back of the eye. That way, we see a bigger image, including the details.

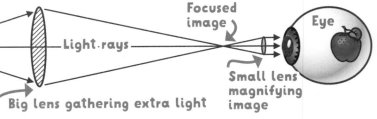

Light rays · Focused image · Eye · Small lens magnifying image · Big lens gathering extra light

☆ LAUGH ATTACK ☆

What do you call a clumsy telescope?

A fell-escope

Knock, knock.
Who's there?
Luke.
Luke who?
Luke through the telescope and you'll see!

What do you get when you cross a telescope with a shell?

A see-shell

What sound does a space turkey make?

Hubble, hubble, hubble

How far can you see on a clear day?

92.96 million miles—from here to the Sun.

STELLAR JIGSAW

Which of these puzzle pieces belong in the numbered spaces?

A

B

C

D

E

BONUS!

Find where the other puzzle pieces belong.

BONUS!

Unscramble the letters below to solve this riddle:
Where do astronauts keep their sandwiches?
NI "CLUNAH" SOBEX!

Where do things that go into a black hole go?

Things that are pulled into the enormous gravity of a black hole become part of it.

Unlike a hole in your sock, a black hole is not an opening; it's a term for a dead star with a very strong gravitational pull. When a big star—much more massive than our Sun—uses up all its fuel after a few million years, it collapses, which means that it squeezes its core tightly together and crushes down to almost nothing. In the small region around this super-dense, super-small object, nothing can escape. Things pulled in by its gravity become part of the compressed mass.

FUN FACT

In April 2019, scientists obtained the first image of a black hole, at the center of the galaxy M87.

This image shows light bending around the intense gravity of the black hole at the center.

Black Hole

SPACE DELIVERY

Pizza's here! Without clues or knowing what to look for, can you find the **23** hidden objects in this scene?

⭐ LAUGH ⭐ ATTACK

What do astronauts wear to bed?
Space jammies

Ryan: Did you hear the joke about the spaceship?
Ally: No.
Ryan: It was out of this world!

Why don't astronauts have to clean up after themselves?
Because space is a vacuum

What do astronauts put on their sandwiches?
Launch meat

Who is Saturn?
The Lord of the Rings

Astronaut #1: Get ready for launch.
Astronaut #2: But I haven't had breakfast yet.

Why did the cow want to be an astronaut?
She wanted to jump over the Moon.

SPEEDY DELIVERY

Try to say these

TONGUE TWISTERS

three times, fast.

**Flora floats faster
than Fauna.**

**Wally walks while
Wyatt waves.**

**Stan's space socks
seem so small.**

ROBOT MAZE

Help the robot roll back to its spaceship. Find a clear path from **START** to **FINISH**. Don't fall into a crater!

START

☆ LAUGH ATTACK ☆

Why did the robot go on vacation?

To recharge its batteries

Why did the robot cross the road?

It was programmed to.

Why was the robot angry?

Someone kept pushing its buttons.

FINISH

UNIDENTIFIED UFOS

UFO usually stands for Unidentified Flying Object. But each of these clues describes a different UFO! Can you identify all the matches?

____ **1.** Large, sad, flightless bird in Paris

____ **2.** Lint-covered breakfast food

____ **3.** Lively international musical

____ **4.** Wise-winged girls in the city

____ **5.** Icy and pristine Atlantic

____ **6.** Unattractive hopping robber

____ **7.** Quickly moving slime

____ **8.** Out-of-the-ordinary sea creature

____ **9.** Hilarious policeman

____ **10.** Parasol party poem

A. Ugly Frog Outlaw

B. Undisturbed Frozen Ocean

C. Unusually Fancy Octopus

D. Umbrella Festival Ode

E. Unhappy French Ostrich

F. Unbelievably Funny Officer

G. Urban Female Owls

H. Untouched Fuzzy Oatmeal

I. Urgently Flowing Ooze

J. Upbeat Foreign Opera

FUN FACT

The National Aviation Reporting Center on Anomalous Phenomena documents and researches aviation-related encounters with UFOs.

NO UFO PARKING

HELP THE CARTOONIST

These cartoons are missing their captions. Write your own punch lines.

Sherlock Holmes and Dr. Watson are on a camping trip. They pitch the tent, then go to sleep. A few hours later, Holmes wakes up his friend.

Holmes: Watson, look up and tell me what you deduce.

Watson: Well, I see millions and millions of stars in the sky. There are likely millions and possibly billions of stars and planets that we haven't even discovered yet.

Holmes: Silly Watson. Our tent has blown away!

ARTSY LOGIC

Cassidy, Matthew, Katie, and Mike created art projects based on planets in the solar system. Using the clues below, can you figure out what art form each student used to create what planet?

	POSTER	DIORAMA	PAPIER-MÂCHÉ	MOSAIC	MERCURY	MARS	JUPITER	NEPTUNE
CASSIDY								
MATTHEW								
KATIE								
MIKE								

Use the chart to keep track of your answers. Put an **X** in each box that can't be true and an **O** in boxes that match.

1. Cassidy used newspaper to create her planet, which is the smallest in the solar system.
2. Katie used found objects to create her art.
3. Mike picked his planet because it's his favorite color—blue.
4. Matthew used a lot of red paint for his project.
5. The Neptune project included its moons in the diorama.

> **What did one planet give to the other for its birthday?**
>
> A ring

Try to say these

☆ **TONGUE TWISTERS** ☆

three times, fast.

Mark makes marker marks.

Pass the purple paint pot, please.

Carly carted crates of crafts.

PLANET PARKING

Help Astronaut Ally find her way back to her spaceship. Once you've found the right path, write the letters along it in order in the spaces below to answer the riddle.

An alien walked up to a parking meter and put in a quarter. "Where's my gum?" he asked.

START

FINISH

How do you have a good outer-space party?

P L _ _ n - E T

BLAST OFF!

Ada is heading to the Moon. Can you find the hidden objects in this scene?

Pretend you are in outer space and an alien is chasing you. What do you do?

¡Buipuətəɹd doʇs

heart

ring

boot

basketball

doughnut

magnifying glass

pencil

baseball bat

Is it tough to break through Earth's atmosphere to get to space?

No, but it takes a huge amount of energy to pull against Earth and enter an orbit around Earth. The craft needs even more energy to leave that path, or orbit, around Earth and go farther out.

The Saturn V rocket used for the Apollo missions in the late 1960s and early 1970s had to create a huge push, or thrust, to put the spacecraft into orbit. The rocket needed so much energy that fuel made up about 90 percent of the total weight. The rocket burned more than 560,000 gallons of fuel in just the first 2¾ minutes after liftoff. To stay in orbit around Earth, the Apollo 11 spacecraft had to go more than 25,000 feet per second. You can imagine that it takes a strong push to get going that fast. To break out of Earth's orbit and head for the Moon, the craft had to go even faster—more than 35,000 feet per second.

That tells you only about the amount of energy needed to escape Earth's gravity. It does not tell you about the many problems that had to be solved to build a craft that could reach those speeds. You can see that it is very tough indeed to escape Earth's gravity.

FUN FACT

Saturn V launched the Apollo 11 mission on July 16, 1969.

This lunar restaurant really has no atmosphere.

SPACE COW

Can you find at least **11** differences between these two pictures?

☆ LAUGH ATTACK ☆

What's an alien's favorite amusement park ride?
The solar coaster

Where does Earth put its clothes?
In the world-robe

Astronaut #1: If you look down, I think you can see China.
Astronaut #2: You've got to be kidding. The next thing I know, you'll tell me I can see knives and forks, too.

Knock, knock.
Who's there?
Mars.
Mars who?
Mars-ipan is a delicious candy confection.

What goes MOOZ?
A spaceship flying backward

The Moon artist was entering her blue period.

Knock, knock.
Who's there?
Jupiter.
Jupiter who?
Jupiter spaceship on my lawn?

Aiden: I'm going to be giving my career report today on being a pilot.
Teacher: Last week you wanted to be an astronaut. What changed your mind?
Aiden: My parents told me that the sky was the limit.

What is interstellar space?

Interstellar space is the space outside our heliosphere.

The heliosphere is a region of space surrounding our solar system. Within the heliosphere, the Sun's solar wind—a constant flow of particles and a magnetic field—affects its surroundings by pushing against particles from other stars and anything that isn't in our solar system. Where the Sun's solar wind stops affecting its surroundings is where the heliosphere ends and where interstellar space begins.

Voyager 1 was the first human-made object to enter interstellar space. It was launched in 1977 and reached interstellar space in August 2012. **Voyager 2**, also launched in 1977, reached interstellar space in November 2018.

FUN FACT

Interstellar space is an almost perfect vacuum.

FUN FACT

Both **Voyager 1** and **Voyager 2** carry a golden record containing sounds and images of life on Earth. They communicate our story to extraterrestrials who might encounter the spacecraft. Both records also have a map to our solar system.

WORD FOR WORDS

The letters in **INTERSTELLAR** can be used to make many other words. Use the clues below to come up with some of them.

INTERSTELLAR

1. A hot drink ___ ___ ___

2. What we breathe ___ ___ ___

3. A snakelike fish ___ ___ ___

4. Someone who doesn't tell the truth ___ ___ ___ ___

5. Water that falls from the sky ___ ___ ___ ___

6. Another word for story ___ ___ ___ ___

7. Extraterrestrial ___ ___ ___ ___ ___

8. To begin ___ ___ ___ ___ ___

9. A baby's toy ___ ___ ___ ___ ___ ___

10. A special ability ___ ___ ___ ___ ___ ___

Write the highlighted letters in the same-colored spaces below to solve the riddle.

What creature in space is really, really slow?

___ ___ ___ ___ ___ ___ ___ ___

PLENTY OF MOONS

Saturn has a lot of moons—over **50** of them! There are **21** of them hidden in the grid. Look for them up, down, across, and diagonally. After you've circled them all, write the leftover letters in order from left to right and top to bottom. They will spell out the answer to the riddle on page 101. We've circled the first word to get you started.

What did one of Saturn's moon's say to the other?

"Let's go for a spin."

~~Aegaeon~~	Fenrir	Pandora
Atlas	Helene	Phoebe
Bestla	Hyperion	Prometheus
Calypso	Janus	Rhea
Dione	Kari	Tarvos
Enceladus	Mimas	Titan
Farbauti	Narvi	Ymir

A	E	G	A	E	O	N	S	A	L	T	A
T	I	S	U	N	A	J	M	I	M	A	S
S	T	I	V	R	A	N	A	T	I	T	H
E	U	S	U	E	H	T	E	M	O	R	P
B	A	D	E	C	K	D	N	C	B	O	A
E	B	W	A	A	A	O	I	E	W	S	N
O	R	E	R	L	I	L	S	O	O	A	D
H	A	I	N	R	E	T	Y	V	N	R	O
P	F	S	E	E	L	C	R	P	I	E	R
O	N	P	V	A	L	A	N	M	S	A	A
C	Y	A	T	I	T	E	Y	E	O	O	N
H	R	I	R	N	E	F	H	A	E	H	R

How many rings are around Saturn?

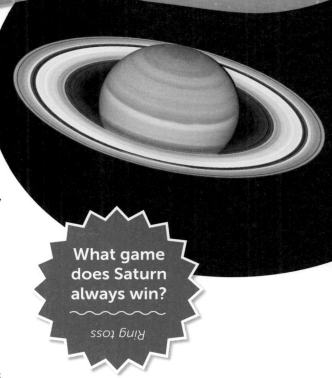

An instrument aboard the Voyager 2 spacecraft counted about 1,000 ringlets in the Saturnian system. The rings are divided into seven major groups, but in photographs we usually see only the three brightest rings.

The rings are mostly made up of small ice particles that move in orbit together. No one is sure where the particles came from. Maybe they were left over after the planet formed, or maybe they split off from a comet was captured by Saturn's gravity. Either way, the rings are thin, probably not any thicker than a house, but the whole set of rings (including the faint, wide ones) forms a racetrack around the planet that's more than 250,000 miles wide.

What game does Saturn always win?

Ring toss

We've known about Saturn's rings for more than 300 years. In the 1970s and 1980s, we were surprised to discover that the other giant planets—Jupiter, Uranus, and Neptune—also have rings around them. But these rings are much fainter than Saturn's.

Why did the sheep jump over the Moon?

Because ____ ____ ____ ____ ____ ____ ____

____ ____ ____ ____ ____ ____ ____ ____

☆ LAUGH ATTACK ☆

What did the astronomer do when she won the lottery?
She thanked her lucky stars!

Which dinosaur loves astronomy?
Sky-ceratops

What do aliens wear to weddings?
Space suits

What do you call a sick extraterrestrial?
An ailin' alien

Why did the astronomer order a double-decker hamburger?
He wanted a meteor burger.

What did the alien say to the garden?
Take me to your weeder!

Knock, knock.
Who's there?
Dee.
Dee who?
Dee stars are in dee sky.

Why don't aliens eat clowns?
Because they taste funny

How do stars start a race?
"Ready, set, glow!"

What do astronomers like to eat?
Quasar-dillas

Can you find 25 CRESCENT MOONS hidden in this scene?

TIC TAC ROW

Each of these aliens has something in common with the other two aliens in the same row—across, down, and diagonally. For example, in the top row across, all three aliens have a UFO behind them. Can you tell what's alike in each row?

LUNAR JIGSAW

Which of these puzzle pieces belong in the numbered spaces?

BONUS!
Find where the other puzzle pieces belong.

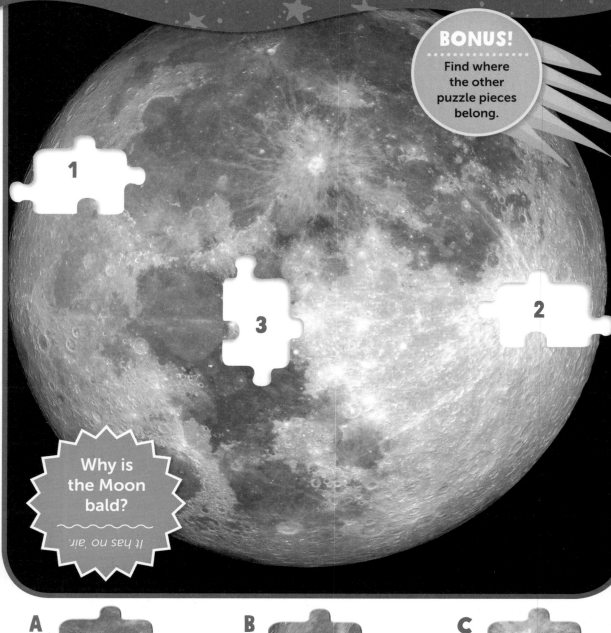

1

3

2

Why is the Moon bald?

It has no 'air'.

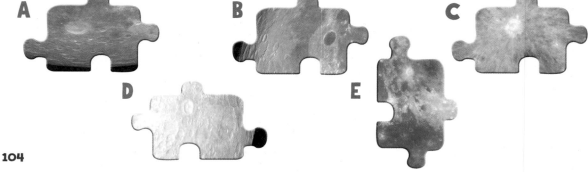

A

B

C

D

E

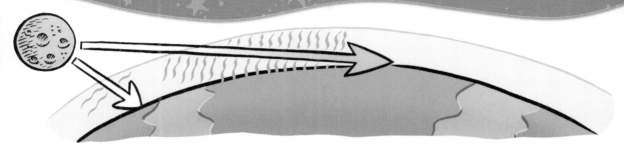

Why is the Moon sometimes yellow?

Earth's air can make the Moon look different colors.

When the Moon first comes up, its light takes a long path through the atmosphere before it reaches you. In that long path, there are lots of particles that scatter light.

Since blue light is scattered more than other colors, some of the blue light from the Moon is taken away. The light that is left for your eye to see has more yellow than other colors. If the air happens to have a lot of dust or pollution, even more light will be absorbed. Then the Moon will look orange or red.

When the Moon is high in the sky, its light has a much shorter path through the atmosphere. Then not as much blue is scattered and lost, so you see the Moon in almost its true color.

Why can you dimly see the rest of the Moon when it is a crescent?

When we see that effect, Earth is reflecting sunlight onto the dark side of the Moon. We call that soft light Earthshine.

Earthshine is brightest just before and after the New Moon, when the Moon is between Earth and the Sun. If people ever live on the Moon, that's when they will see a "Full Earth." The side of Earth that's facing them will be big and bright, completely lit by the Sun.

What did Neptune say to its largest moon?

"You Triton my day."

SPACE WALK

Carter is having a blast in space! Can you find the hidden objects in this scene?

button

pencil

suitcase

slice of pizza

eyeglasses

party hat

sock

What was the first animal in space?

The cow that jumped over the Moon.

What fish comes out at night?

Starfish

balloon

umbrella

belt

envelope

spatula

wedge of lime

crown

ghost

horseshoe

ruler

drinking straw

BOOKS NEVER WRITTEN

Check out the titles of these **10** funny books. See how many you can match with the author. **(Hint: Try reading the authors' names out loud!)**

H 1. *Distance to the Moon*

___ 2. *A Biography of Jupiter*

___ 3. *My Life in Outer Space*

___ 4. *Proof of Extraterrestrials*

___ 5. *Did You See the Lights?*

___ 6. *Identify Constellations*

___ 7. *Weather in Space*

___ 8. *Space Radiation*

___ 9. *How to Save the Planet*

___ 10. *Floating Furniture*

A. A. Leon Being

B. Vera E. Cold

C. Reese Ickle

D. Aunty Gravity

E. Leo O. Ryan

F. Co. S. Mick Ray

G. I. Malone

H. Myles A. Way

I. Aurora B. Ellias

J. Ima Giant

SCRAMBLED SPACE

There are **5** objects hidden in this cartoon. Unscramble the words to figure out the hidden objects, then find them in the scene!

What's the Red Planet's favorite song?

"Mars and Stripes Forever"

PEPRA ILCP ___ ___ ___ ___ ___ ___ ___ ___ ___

EKASN ___ ___ ___ ___ ___

CSOREC LBAL ___ ___ ___ ___ ___ ___ ___ ___ ___

HTSBHOROTU ___ ___ ___ ___ ___ ___ ___ ___ ___ ___

LTETUR ___ ___ ___ ___ ___ ___

SPACE SHUTTLE LAUNCH

Can you find at least **17** differences between these two photos?

FUN FACT

The word *astronaut* is derived from Greek words meaning "star sailor."

Which planet circles the Sun the fastest?

Mercury, the planet closest to the Sun, has the fastest orbit of all the planets. It circles the Sun every 88 days. In fact, in any solar system, the closest planet must always be the fastest.

A star's pull is stronger close to the star than it is farther away. So only planets that are orbiting fast enough to resist this stronger pull of gravity will stay in orbit and not fall into the star.

FUN FACT

The fastest planet has the same name as the messenger-god in Roman mythology.

☆ LAUGH ATTACK ☆

What do pizza and Earth have in common?
They both have crusts.

Noah: Why are you so happy?
Chloe: The rotation of Earth really makes my day.

What did one alien say to another after he returned from vacation?
"Where on Earth have you been?"

Where can planets update their status?
Their space-book account

Emma: How fast does light travel?
Ethan: I don't know—it's already arrived by the time I wake up.

How do you get around in space?
By galaxy cab

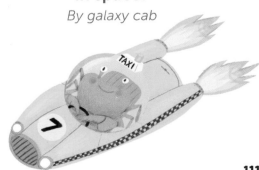

WHAT'S WRONG?

Which things in this picture are silly? It's up to you!

☆ LAUGH ATTACK ☆

What sends tennis balls into space?

Tennis rockets

What do you call a sick planet?

Strep-tune

Stephanie: Triangulum Australe is the longest constellation name. How do you spell it?
Patrick: T-R-I-A-N-G-U-L-U-M A-U-S-T-R-A-L-E.
Stephanie: No, *it* is spelled I-T.

What is at the end of the Milky Way?

The letter Y

Can Saturn take a bath?

Yes, but it will leave a ring around the tub.

Dad: Why did you get a zero on your test?
Jake: That's not a zero. That's the Moon. The teacher ran out of stars.

How many balls of string would it take to reach the Moon?

Just one, but it would have to be a big one.

Where do you find black holes?

It depends on where you lost them!

Why was the astronomer's head wet?

She had a brainstorm.

Why did the cow go to space?

It wanted to see the moooooon.

What do you call a spaceship that drips water?

A crying saucer

STARGAZING

There are **14** stars shining in the grids below.
Here's how to figure out where they belong:

- Each numbered square tells you how many
  of the empty squares touching it (above, below,
  left, right, or diagonally) contain a star.

- Place an **X** on squares that can't
  have a star. Draw a star on squares
  that have one.

Hints:

- A star cannot go in a square
  that has a number.

- Even if you're not sure where to
  put all the stars around a number,
  fill in the ones you are sure of.

- Keep trying possibilities with
  a pencil and eraser!

1			
2			1
		4	
1		3	

	3		1		
					1
		2			2
	2	2	2		1
		2			
3				1	

How does a star form?

That's an important question, since our light, warmth, and food energy come from a nearby star that we call the Sun.

Stars form in clouds of gas and dust floating in space. Over many years, the small pull of gravity between those bits of gas and dust brings them together into clumps. In time, one clump gathers enough material to become a big ball.

The weight of the outer material makes the pressure at the center of the ball very high. Under this pressure, bits of gas and dust begin to hit one another, heating up the center. The heat breaks down the gas and dust into smaller bits called atoms.

The ball pulls in more material. It grows larger. Under higher pressure, the center gets even hotter. The heat strips away the outer parts of the atoms and leaves only the heavy central parts, called nuclei (NUKE-lee-eye).

Barnard 68, the space cloud shown here, is in our galaxy. It is more than 20 million times as far from us as the Sun.

The cloud looks black because its dust particles block light from stars in the distance.

Its temperature is −440°F. That's hundreds of degrees colder than the North Pole.

This dark bulge is where a smaller cloud is bumping into the main cloud. The pressure may be enough to collapse them.

This space cloud is made of gases with some dust. Gravity holds the gaseous cloud together.

The center of the ball gets hotter than anything we can experience on Earth, except in special machines. The nuclei bang together so hard that they break into pieces, which then come together to form bigger nuclei. This nuclear reaction releases huge amounts of energy, including light and heat. And a star is born.

☆ LAUGH ATTACK ☆

When did that get here?

What's the first day of the week called in outer space?
Moon-day

What happens when astronauts misbehave?
They get grounded.

What's an astronaut's favorite dance?
The moonwalk

What did Venus say to Saturn?
Give me a ring sometime!

Why was the sea otter on the spaceship?
To get to otter space

Which of these two rockets are the same?

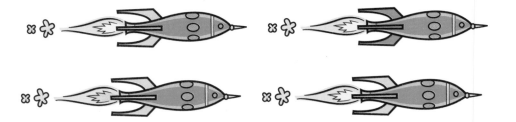

Can you find 25 MAGNETS hidden in this scene?

MISSION: DECODE

There have been multiple NASA missions that sent humans into space. Use the list of manned missions to solve this puzzle. Each coded space has two numbers. The first number tells you which mission to look at. The second number tells you which letter in that mission to use. For example, the first coded letter is **1-4**. The **1** tells you to go to **MERCURY**. Look **4** letters in, and you've got a **C**. Fill in the rest to decode these space jokes.

1. MERCURY
2. GEMINI
3. APOLLO
4. SKYLAB
5. APOLLO-SOYUZ
6. SPACE SHUTTLE
7. INTERNATIONAL SPACE STATION

What's an astronaut's favorite reindeer?

C ___ ___ ___ ___
1-4 3-3 2-3 2-2 6-9

What do astronauts like to eat for lunch?

___ ___ ___ ___ - ___ ___ ___ ___
4-1 5-3 1-5 3-2   7-1 7-3 6-5 1-3

What do you call the lights on a spaceship?

___ ___ ___ ___ ___ ___ ___ ___ ___
2-3 7-10 3-3 7-6 4-6 6-12 3-1 1-1 5-7

117

KIDS' SCIENCE QUESTIONS

How did the stars get grouped into galaxies?

Scientists think stars are grouped into galaxies because that is where the stars formed.

Every galaxy began as a huge cloud of gas and dust. Each molecule of gas and each bit of dust has its own weak gravity. So the gas and dust pulled together into clumps, and in those clumps, stars formed. These clouds were very large and led to the creation of billions of stars. In fact, that process is still happening. The Milky Way (the galaxy we live in) continues to create a few new stars every year.

New stars are still forming in this cloud of gas and dust.

GALAXY MATCH

There are three main types of galaxies. Based on the name and description, can you match the galaxy type with the correct photo?

_____ **SPIRAL:** a flat disk with a central bulge and spiral arms

_____ **ELLIPTICAL:** round or oval shaped

_____ **IRREGULAR:** no identifiable shape or structure

GALAXIES GALORE

Each of the galaxies below is missing its vowels. Can you figure out the names of these galaxies?

1. NDRMD ＿ ＿ ＿ ＿ ＿ ＿ ＿ ＿

2. NDL ＿ ＿ ＿ ＿ ＿ ＿

3. HCKY STCK ＿ ＿ ＿ ＿ ＿ ＿ ＿   ＿ ＿ ＿ ＿ ＿

4. TDPL ＿ ＿ ＿ ＿ ＿ ＿

5. WHRLPL ＿ ＿ ＿ ＿ ＿ ＿ ＿ ＿

6. FRWRKS ＿ ＿ ＿ ＿ ＿ ＿ ＿ ＿

7. BLK Y ＿ ＿ ＿ ＿ ＿   ＿ ＿ ＿

8. MLKY WY ＿ ＿ ＿ ＿ ＿   ＿ ＿ ＿

9. SNFLWR ＿ ＿ ＿ ＿ ＿ ＿ ＿ ＿ ＿

10. CRTWHL ＿ ＿ ＿ ＿ ＿ ＿ ＿ ＿ ＿

FUN FACT

Galaxies are relatively close together, so neighboring galaxies occasionally merge. The Milky Way and Andromeda galaxies will merge in about 4 billion years.

HERE COMES THE SUN

This puzzle is so bright, you're gonna need shades. Circle the **29** words in this grid that contain the word **SUN**. The word **SUN** has been replaced with a ☀. Look up, down, across, backward, and diagonally. The uncircled letters answer the trivia question.

WORD LIST

SUNBAKED
SUNBATHE
SUNBEAM
SUNBLOCK
SUNBURN
SUNBURNED
SUNDAE
SUNDAY
SUNDECK
SUNDIAL

SUNDOWN
SUNDRESS
SUNFISH
SUNKEN
SUNLIGHT
SUNLIT
SUNNIER
SUNNY
SUNRAY
SUNRISE

SUNROOF
SUNROOM
SUNSCREEN
SUNSET
SUNSHINE
SUNSPOT
SUNTAN
TSUNAMI
UNSUNG

TRIVIA QUESTION:

If the Sun were the size of a door in your house, how big would Earth be? Put the uncircled letters in order on the blanks.

ANSWER:

__ __ __ __ __ __ __ __ __ __

__ __ __ __ __ __

☆ LAUGH ATTACK ☆

How do you know the Sun is smart?
It's so bright.

What holds the Sun up in the sky?
Sunbeams

What did the Sun say when it went up on stage?
"This is my time to shine."

How did the astronaut serve lemonade?
In sunglasses

121

☆ LAUGH ATTACK ☆

Which astronaut wears the biggest helmet?

The one with the biggest head

How do astronauts brush their teeth?

With tooth-space

What do you get when you cross a kangaroo and an alien?

A Mars-upial

Astronaut #1: I'm going to the Sun.
Astronaut #2: You can't. It's too hot.
Astronaut #1: Then I'll go at night.

How do astronauts serve their food?

With a Big Dipper

Why did the astronaut try to eat a star?

Because he wanted a light snack

Knock, knock.
Who's there?
Juana.
Juana who?
Juana go to the Moon?

How do astronauts keep their pants up?

With an asteroid belt

Why did the astronaut get a ticket?

She broke the law of gravity.

Astronaut #1: There's an asteroid at two o'clock!
Astronaut #2: Roger that. Would that be AM or PM?

FLOATING IN SPACE

To find the answer to the riddle below, first cross out all the pairs of matching letters. Then write the remaining letters in order in the spaces beneath the riddle.

FUN FACT

The International Space Station orbits Earth 16 times in 24 hours.

What was the name of the first satellite to orbit Earth?

The Moon

FF	NN	GR	BB	II	WW
LL	AV	VV	DD	MM	KK
CC	HH	SS	OO	IS	ZZ
AA	TT	EA	RR	JJ	XX

Where can you go snorkeling in space?

In the ___ ___ ___ ___ – ___ ___ ___

123

WORD FOR WORDS

The letters in **SPACE STATION** can be used to make many other words. Use the clues below to come up with some of them.

SPACE STATION

----

1. A feline   ____ ____ ____

2. Frozen water   ____ ____ ____

3. A short sleep   ____ ____ ____

4. The direction opposite of west   ____ ____ ____ ____

5. Where birds keep their eggs   ____ ____ ____ ____

6. Used to wash something   ____ ____ ____ ____

7. Another word for *shore*   ____ ____ ____ ____

8. A long, narrow boat   ____ ____ ____ ____ ____

9. The year has four of them   ____ ____ ____ ____ ____

10. An ant is one   ____ ____ ____ ____ ____ ____

Write the highlighted letters in the same-colored spaces below to solve the riddle.

What did one rocket ship say to the other?

Give me some ____ ____ ____ ____ ____ .

LIFE IN SPACE

Astronauts from multiple countries live and work on the International Space Station (ISS), which orbits Earth. Learn about life aboard the ISS from NASA astronaut **Dr. Karen Nyberg**, who has spent a total of 180 days in space.

What do astronauts do on the ISS?
We do science experiments on ourselves to study how the human body reacts to being away from Earth's gravity. We also do a ton of experiments ranging from growing plants from seeds to fire experiments to different fluid experiments. We'll have anywhere from 100 to 150 different experiments going on at one time.

How much free time do you have?
On weekdays it was hard to find free time. On Saturdays, we spent most of the morning cleaning, then the afternoon was free. But we also exercised two hours a day, so after you cleaned and did your exercise, there wasn't much time. Sunday was usually the day when I could fit in a hobby. I brought up some sewing, but I didn't have much time to do it.

How was the food?
Our food was great. We have a large variety. My favorite was the red beans and rice, which is in a foil packet. Spicy!

Why do you have to exercise on the ISS?
Our bodies adapt to the environment we're in. And so, when you don't have gravity, you don't need as much bone strength or muscle strength because you're not standing upright or lifting things. Your heart doesn't need to be as strong because it takes less effort to pump blood. That would be fine if you were going to live in space the rest of your life, but we have to come back to Earth and gravity.

What's the funniest thing that happened?
We had fun playing silly zero-gravity games. We would start at one end of the Space Station and try to push off and make it as far as possible without hitting the walls. I was really, really bad at it! You're trying to move your body without touching anything, which—it's just funny to watch.

WHAT'S WRONG?

Which things in this picture are silly? It's up to you!

☆ LAUGH ATTACK ☆

Where are black holes most commonly found?
In black socks

What game do you play at an outer-space party?
Pin the tail on the comet

What did the alien say to the cat?
Take me to your litter.

What do Moon people do when they get married?
Go on their honey-earth!

What do a telephone and Saturn both have in common?
They both ring, ring, ring.

How do you measure an astronaut for a space suit?
From their head to their Plu-toes.

NAVIGATION'S A GO!

Voyager Dusk is blasting off to Planet Zatz. To get there, the ship must first pass through planets Zoom and Zorka. Can you get it there while avoiding the black hole?

What does outer space have in common with basketball?

They both have shooting stars.

START

BLACK HOLE

FINISH

What's a light-year?

The same as a regular year, but with fewer calories.

JUPITER JIGSAW

Which of these puzzle pieces belong in the numbered spaces?

1

2

3

BONUS!
Find where the other puzzle pieces belong.

What's at the center of Jupiter?

The letter i

A

B

C

D

E

CRISSCROSS MOON

Jupiter has **79** moons. Fifteen of them are listed below. Each will fit into the grid in only one way. Use the number of letters in each word as a clue to where it might fit. We started you off with **ERSA**. Once you fill them in, unscramble the highlighted letters to find the answer to the riddle.

2 Letters
IO

4 Letters
ERSA
KALE
LEDA

5 Letters
CARPO
THEBE

6 Letters
EUROPA
KALYKE
PANDIA

7 letters
CYLLENE
HIMALIA

8 Letters
AMALTHEA
CALLISTO
GANYMEDE
ORTHOSIE

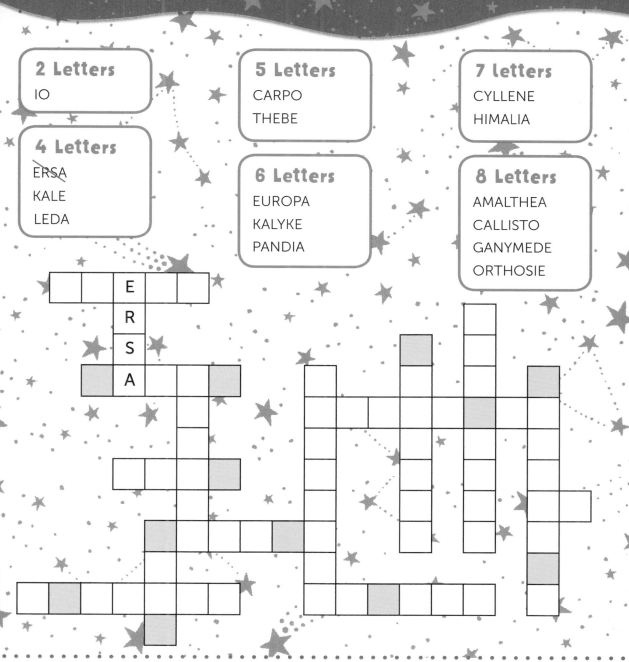

What kind of chicken can fly to the Moon?

_ _ _ _ _ _ _ _ _ _ _ _ _

SCRAMBLED SPACE

There are **5** objects hidden in this cartoon. Unscramble the letters to figure out the hidden objects, then find them in the scene!

What did the kids say about the field trip to the planetarium?

"It was out of this world!"

SCHOOL BUS

INTERSTELLAR ELEMENTARY

NAANAB _ _ _ _ _ _

TEANPHEL _ _ _ _ _ _ _ _

SUMIC RAPEYL _ _ _ _ _ _ _ _ _ _ _

CENPIL _ _ _ _ _ _

RESTOAT _ _ _ _ _ _ _

KIDS' SCIENCE QUESTIONS

Get back here!

Can you yo-yo in space?

Yes, you can. Astronauts did it.

On Earth, if we loop the string over a finger and let the yo-yo drop, gravity pulls the toy downward. The string unwinds, causing the yo-yo to spin. We can use the downward energy and spinning energy of the yo-yo to do tricks. But to do them, we have to throw the yo-yo to keep it going against gravity.

In space, astronauts did not have gravity. If they let go of the yo-yo, it floated in place. They had to throw it to make it unwind at all. Once they threw it, they could easily do lots of fancy tricks. In fact, they could "throw" the yo-yo gently and do tricks more slowly than we can do them on Earth.

There was one trick they couldn't do. They couldn't make the yo-yo "sleep," or spin at the end of its string. Without gravity, they could not get the right tension in the string to keep the yo-yo from winding back up.

What happens to tears or nose drips in space?

Because of low gravity in space, an astronaut's tears don't fall. Instead, they form a blob of water that stays on the eye or cheek until it's wiped away.

Other fluids move differently in low gravity, too. Astronauts get stuffy noses when they arrive in space, and their heads look and feel puffy. That's because blood and other fluids aren't pulled down in their bodies as they are in Earth's gravity. Astronauts deal with a stuffy head in space the same way they do on Earth: by blowing their nose. They just may need to do it a bit more often.

REACH FOR THE STARS

"Twinkle, twinkle, little puzzle." Circle the **30** words or phrases containing **STAR** hidden in this grid. The word **STAR** has been replaced with a ⭐. Look up, down, across, backward, and diagonally. The uncircled letters answer the trivia question.

WORD LIST

CORNSTARCH
CUSTARD
DASTARDLY
KICK-START
LODESTAR
LUCKY STARS
MEGASTAR
MOVIE STAR
MUSTARD
POLESTAR
ROCK STAR

STAR ANISE
STAR MAP
STAR FRUIT
STAR POWER
STAR-STUDDED
STARBOARD
STARBURST
STARDOM
STARDUST
STARFISH
STARGAZE

STARLIGHT
STARLING
STARSHIP
STARSTRUCK
STARTUP
STARVE
SUPERSTAR
WISH UPON
A STAR

TRIVIA QUESTION:

What is a shooting star?
Put the uncircled letters in order on the blanks.

ANSWER:

It __ __ __'__ __ __ __ __ __ __ __

__ __ __. __ __'__ __ __ __ __ __ __ __.

132

☆ LAUGH ATTACK ☆

What's a star's favorite game?
Hide-and-glow-seek

What keeps stars cool?
Their fans

How did the astronaut's mom know he didn't clean his room?
There was a lot of stardust everywhere.

Why did the astronomer want to go to Hollywood?
To see the stars

```
★ B O A R D I D A ★ D L Y
E T H G I L ★ ★ S H I P P
D T S N S U P E R ★ O A T
O ★ L U C K Y ★ S L M A R
L K A ★ A N I S E ★ D O ★
T C K N S T A ★ R E C F D
R I C T O A T A D K I ★ H
E K U S S P E D ★ S U L C
W ★ R R L U U Z H M I M ★
O L T U F T D H A T E S N
P I S B S ★ A ★ S G V M R
★ N ★ ★ ★ D O M A I ★ E O
T G M O V I E ★ E O W R C
```

THE LAST LAUGH

SNORK SNORK!

These jokes are out of this world!

Meghan: Why are you so tired today?
Madison: I was up all night waiting for the Sun to come up, but then it dawned on me.

Why didn't the constellation laugh at the joke?
It was too Sirius.

What type of party did the otter throw for his birthday?
An otter-space party

What did the astronaut get when he went mini-golfing?
A black hole in one

Josh: What's the last letter in galaxy?
Livi: Y.
Josh: Because I want to know for my space report.

What do you call a shark in space?
Lost

Syri: Which is farther—New York City or the Moon?
Alex: New York City.
Syri: Why do you say that?
Alex: I can see the Moon, but I can't see New York City.

Eep Eep!

How do you spell Cassiopeia backward?
C-A-S-S-I-O-P-E-I-A B-A-C-K-W-A-R-D

Knock, knock.
Who's there?
Shirley.
Shirley who?
Shirley this is the last space joke.

BLURF BLURF!

ANSWERS

Page 2

MERCURY
VENUS
EARTH
MARS
JUPITER
SATURN
URANUS
NEPTUNE

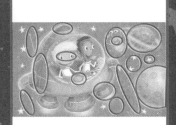

SATURN **JUPITER** **MARS** **EARTH**

Page 3

Pages 4-5

Page 9

Page 10

	x	3	
2			2
x	2	x	x
0	x	x	0

	1	x	x	x	1
x	x	x	2	x	
2				x	1
x		6		4	x
x	x	x			2
0	x	1	x	3	

Page 11

Zig: Hot Planet;
Red Ship
Vot: Cold Planet;
Blue Ship
Spo: Wet Planet;
Yellow Ship

Pages 12-13

WE CAME IN PEACE
FOR ALL MANKIND

Page 14

1. DAM
2. EAR
3. OAR
4. MARE
5. MEND
6. ADORE
7. AROMA
8. MADRE
9. RAMEN
10. RANDOM

Page 15

ANSWERS

Page 17

1. A
2. A
3. B
4. A
5. A
6. B
7. A

Pages 18–19

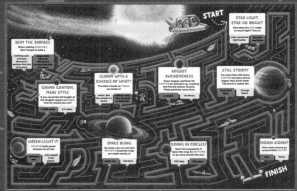

Page 21

April **LYRIDS**
August **PERSEIDS**
October **ORIONIDS**
November **LEONIDS**
December **GEMINIDS**
December/January
QUADRANTIDS

Page 22

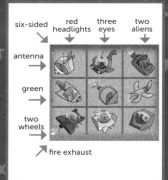

Page 23

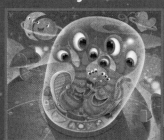

What did the three-eyed
alien say to her sweetheart?
"EYE, EYE, EYE LOVE YOU."

Pages 24–25

Pages 26–27

ANSWERS

Page 28

Pages 30-31

Why did the astronaut smile during takeoff?

IT WAS A BLAST.

Page 32

Pages 34-35

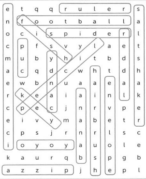

Page 37

1. ECLIPSE
2. JUPITER
3. PLANET
4. GALAXY
5. SATURN
6. BLACK HOLE
7. SOLAR FLARE
8. SOLAR SYSTEM
9. COMET
10. BIG DIPPER

How does the solar system tell jokes?

With a lot of STARCASM

Page 39

Pages 42-43

There are more blue stars.

Riddle 1: NOT IN A MILLION YEARS
Riddle 2: YOU ROCKET
Riddle 3: BECAUSE IT WAS FULL
Riddle 4: UNIDENTIFIED FRYING OBJECTS

ANSWERS

Pages 44–45

Pages 46–47

FRYING PAN
SPATULA
SPOON
FUNNEL
SPONGE

Page 48

```
        J O H N Y O U N G
E D G A R M I T C H E L L
        M
D A V I D S C O T T     N
        S         C     E
  H A R R I S O N S C H M I T T
        L       A       L
        I       R       A
        W       B U Z Z A L D R I N
        I       E       M
        N       D       S
P E T E C O N R A D     U   T
        A               K   R
A L A N S H E P A R D       O
                            N
            E U G E N E C E R N A N
```

The space program's
name was APOLLO.

Pages 50–51

Page 54

What did the Sun say
when it was introduced
to Earth?
**"I'M VERY PLEASED
TO HEAT YOU."**

Pages 56–57

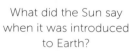

ANSWERS

Page 58

MARS
COMET
SATURN
ORBIT
MILKY WAY
BLACK HOLE
JUPITER
ASTEROID
VENUS

What do you get when you cross a galaxy and a toad?
STAR WARTS

Page 60

Letters: **A C H L N U**

L	U	H	C	N	A
N	A	C	H	U	L
H	N	U	L	A	C
C	L	A	N	H	U
U	H	L	A	C	N
A	C	N	U	L	H

LAUNCH

Page 61

Pages 62-63

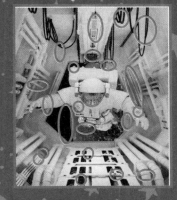

Pages 64-65

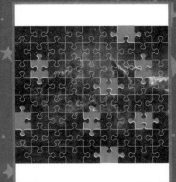

Page 66

Pages 68-69

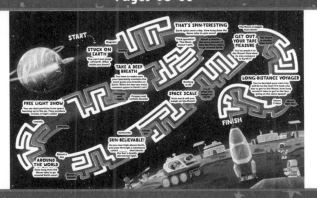

Pages 70-71

What's on the breakfast menu at a space restaurant?
A COMET OMELET

★ ANSWERS

Pages 72-73

What do you call a magician from outer space?
A FLYING SORCERER

What do you call a pecan in a spaceship?
AN ASTRO-NUT

How did the rocket lose its job?
IT GOT FIRED.

Page 74

Page 75

What do Moon people call french fries?
CRATER TATERS

Pages 78-79

Mission control says,
"BLAST OFF!"

Page 80

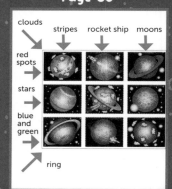

Pages 82-83

ECLIPSE
METEOR
ORBIT
MOON
STAR
SUN

Page 84

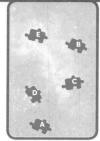

Where do astronauts keep their sandwiches?
IN "LAUNCH" BOXES!

Pages 86-87

ANSWERS

Pages 88-89

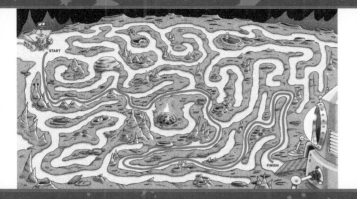

Page 90

1. E
2. H
3. J
4. G
5. B
6. A
7. I
8. C
9. F
10. D

Page 92

Cassidy: papier-mâché; Mercury
Matthew: poster; Mars
Katie: mosaic; Jupiter
Mike: diorama; Neptune

Page 93

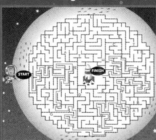

How do you have a good outer-space party?
PLAN-ET

Page 94

Page 96

Page 99

1. TEA
2. AIR
3. EEL
4. LIAR
5. RAIN
6. TALE
7. ALIEN
8. START
9. RATTLE
10. TALENT

What creature in space is really, really slow?
A SNALIEN

Pages 100-101

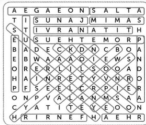

Why did the sheep jump over the Moon?
Because THE COW WAS ON VACATION

ANSWERS

Pages 102-103

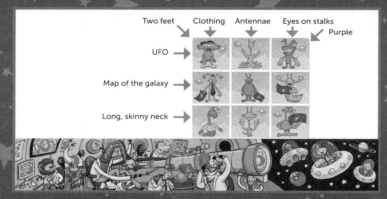

	Two feet / Clothing	Antennae	Eyes on stalks / Purple
UFO			
Map of the galaxy			
Long, skinny neck			

Page 104

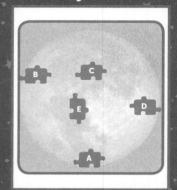

Pages 106-107

Page 108

1. H
2. J
3. G
4. A
5. I
6. E
7. B
8. F
9. C
10. D

Page 109

PAPER CLIP
SNAKE
SOCCER BALL
TOOTHBRUSH
TURTLE

Page 110

Page 114

1	X	X	X
2	★	X	1
X	★	4	★
1	X	3	★

★	3	X	1	X	X
★	★	X	X	★	1
X	X	2	★	X	2
X	2	2	2	★	1
★	★	2	X	X	X
3	★	X	X	1	★

ANSWERS

Pages 116-117

What's an astronaut's favorite reindeer?
COMET
What do astronauts like to eat for lunch?
SOUP-ITER
What do you call the lights on a spaceship?
MOONBEAMS

Page 118

Spiral: C
Elliptical: B
Irregular: A

Page 119

1. ANDROMEDA
2. NEEDLE
3. HOCKEY STICK
4. TADPOLE
5. WHIRLPOOL
6. FIREWORKS
7. BLACK EYE
8. MILKY WAY
9. SUNFLOWER
10. CARTWHEEL

Pages 120-121

Trivia Answer:
THE SIZE OF A NICKEL

Page 123

Where can you go snorkeling in space?
IN THE GRAVI-SEA

Page 124

1. CAT
2. ICE
3. NAP
4. EAST
5. NEST
6. SOAP
7. COAST
8. CANOE
9. SEASON
10. INSECT

What did one rocket ship say to the other?
GIVE ME SOME SPACE.

Page 127

Page 128

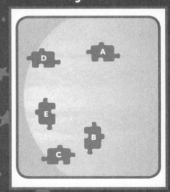

ANSWERS

Page 129

What kind of chicken
can fly to the Moon?
A ROCKET CHICK

Page 130

BANANA
ELEPHANT
MUSIC PLAYER
PENCIL
TOASTER

Pages 132–133

Trivia Answer:
**IT ISN'T A STAR AT ALL.
IT'S A METEOR.**

Photo Credits:

1971yes/Getty (62–63); alex_skp/iStock/Getty Images Plus (131); bezov/iStock (24–25); ClaudioVentrella/Getty (64–65); ClaudioVentrella/iStock (70–71, 132–133); ESA/Hubble & NASA (119); ESO (115); ESO/EHT Collaboration (85); European Space Agency & NASA (118); Jupiterimages Corporation (48); NASA (2, 43, 45, 95, 98, 110, 118, 124, 125); NASA Goddard (55, 104); NASA, ESA, A. Simon (Goddard Space Flight Center), and M. H. Wong (University of California, Berkeley) (101); NASA, ESA, and A. Aloisi (European Space Agency and Space Telescope Science Institute) (118); NASA, ESA, the Hubble Heritage Team (STScI/AURA), A. Nola (ESA/STScI), and the Westerlund 2 Science Team (84); NASA, Holland Ford (JHU), the ACS Science Team and ESA (119); NASA, ESA, R. M. Crockett (University of Oxford, U.K.), S. Kaviraj (Imperial College London and University of Oxford, U.K.), J. Silk (University of Oxford), M. Mutchler (Space Telescope Science Institute, Baltimore, USA), R. O'Connell (University of Virginia, Charlottesville, USA), and the WFC3 Scientific Oversight Committee (118); NASA/ESA and The Hubble Heritage Team (AURA/STScI) (119); NASA/JPL (37); NASA/JPL/Space Science Institute (128); NASA/JPL/USGS (37); NASA/JPL-Caltech (14, 59, 81, 98); Nomad/SuperStock (4–5); subjug/iStock/Getty Images Plus (131); Tevecoleimages/iStock (114); Yuri Arcurs Media/SuperStock (4–5)

For information about permission to reprint selections from
this book, please contact permissions@highlights.com.

Published by Highlights Press
815 Church Street
Honesdale, Pennsylvania 18431
ISBN: 978-1-64472-125-4
Manufactured in Dongguan, Guangdong, China
Mfg. 06/2020

First edition
Visit our website at Highlights.com.
10 9 8 7 6 5 4 3 2 1